Charles Kingsley

The gospel of the Pentateuch

a set of parish sermons ; and David

Charles Kingsley

The gospel of the Pentateuch
 a set of parish sermons ; and David

ISBN/EAN: 9783744744690

Printed in Europe, USA, Canada, Australia, Japan

Cover: Foto ©Thomas Meinert / pixelio.de

More available books at **www.hansebooks.com**

THE GOSPEL

OF THE PENTATEUCH

A SET OF PARISH SERMONS

AND

DAVID

FIVE SERMONS.

BY THE
REV. CHARLES KINGSLEY,
LATE RECTOR OF EVERSLEY AND CANON OF WESTMINSTER.

London:
MACMILLAN & CO.
1878.

CONTENTS.

CONTENTS.

SERMON VII.

CONTENTS

PREFACE TO THE FIRST EDITION

OF

THE GOSPEL OF THE PENTATEUCH.

TO THE REV. CANON STANLEY.

MY DEAR STANLEY,

I dedicate these Sermons to you, not that I may make you responsible for any doctrine or statement contained in them, but as the simplest method of telling you how much they owe to your book on the Jewish Church, and of expressing my deep gratitude to you for publishing that book at such a time as this.

It has given to me (and I doubt not to many other clergymen) a fresh confidence and energy in preaching to my people the Gospel of the Old Testament as the same with that of the New;

and without it, many of these Sermons would have been very different from, and I am certain very inferior to, what they are now, by the help of your admirable book.

Brought up, like all Cambridge men of the last generation, upon Paley's *Evidences*, I had accepted as a matter of course, and as the authoritative teaching of my University, Paley's opinions as to the limits of Biblical criticism,* quoted at large in Dean Milman's noble preface to his last edition of the *History of the Jews;* and especially that great dictum of his, 'that it is an unwarrantable, as well as unsafe rule to lay down concerning the Jewish history, that which was never laid down concerning any other, that either every particular of it must be true, or the whole false.'

I do not quote the rest of the passage; first, because you, I doubt not, know it as well as I; and next, in order that if any one shall read these lines who has not read Paley's *Evidences*, he may be stirred up to look the passage out for himself,

* *Evidences*, Part III. Cap. iii.

and so become acquainted with a great book and a great mind.

A reverent and rational liberty in criticism (within the limits of orthodoxy) is, I have always supposed, the right of every Cambridge man; and I was therefore the more shocked, for the sake of free thought in my University, at the appearance of a book which claimed and exercised a licence in such questions, which I must (after careful study of it) call anything but rational and reverent. Of the orthodoxy of the book it is not, of course, a private clergyman's place to judge. That book seemed dangerous to the University of Cambridge itself, because it was likely to stir up from without attempts to abridge her ancient liberty of thought; but it seemed still more dangerous to the hundreds of thousands without the University, who, being no scholars, must take on trust the historic truth of the Bible.

For I found that book, if not always read, yet still talked and thought of on every side, among persons whom I should have fancied careless of its subject, and even ignorant of its existence, but to whom I was personally bound to give some answer as to the book and its worth. It was making many unsettled and unhappy; it was (even worse) pandering to the cynicism and frivolity of many who were already too cynical and frivolous; and, much as I shrank from descending into the arena of religious controversy, I felt bound to say a few plain words on it, at least to my own parishioners.

But how to do so, without putting into their heads thoughts which need be in no man's head, and perhaps shaking the very faith which I was trying to build up, was difficult to me, and I think would have been impossible to me, but for the opportune appearance of your admirable book.

I could not but see that the book to which I have alluded, like most other modern books on Biblical criticism, was altogether negative; was possessed too often by that fanaticism of disbelief which is just as dangerous as the fanaticism of belief;

was picking the body of the Scripture to pieces
so earnestly, that it seemed to forget that Scripture had a spirit as well as a body; or, if it
confessed that it had a spirit, asserting that spirit
to be one utterly different from the spirit which
the Scripture asserts that it possesses.

For the Scripture asserts that those who wrote
it were moved by the Spirit of God; that it is a
record of God's dealings with men, which certain
men were inspired to perceive and to write down:
whereas the tendency of modern criticism is, without doubt, to assert that Scripture is inspired by
the spirit of man; that it contains the thoughts
and discoveries of men concerning God, which
they wrote down without the inspiration of God;
which difference seems to me (and I hope to
others) utterly infinite and incalculable, and to
involve the question of the whole character,
honour, and glory of God.

There is, without a doubt, something in the
Old Testament, as well as in the New, quite
different in kind, as well as in degree, from the

sacred books of any other people: an unique
element, which has had an unique effect upon
the human heart, life and civilization. This remains, after all possible deductions for 'ignorance
of physical science,' 'errors in numbers and chron-
ology,' 'interpolations,' 'mistakes of transcribers,'
and so forth, whereof we have read of late a great
deal too much, and ought to care for them and
for their existence, or non-existence, simply nothing at all; because, granting them all—though
the greater part of them I do not grant, as far
as I can trust my critical faculty—there remains
that unique element, beside which all these accidents are but as the spots on the sun compared to
the great glory of his life-giving light. The unique
element is there; and I cannot but still believe,
after much thought, that it—the powerful and
working element, the inspired and Divine element
which has converted and still converts millions
of souls—is just that which Christendom in all
ages has held it to be: the account of certain
'noble acts' of God's, and not of certain noble

thoughts of man—in a word, not merely the moral, but the historic element; and that, therefore, the value of the Bible teaching depends on the truth of the Bible story. That is my belief. Any criticism which tries to rob me of that I shall look at fairly, but very severely indeed.

If all that a man wants is a 'religion,' he ought to be able to make a very pretty one for himself, and a fresh one as often as he is tired of the old. But the heart and soul of man wants more than that, as it is written, 'My soul is athirst for God, even for the living God.' Those whom I have to teach want a living God, who cares for men, works for men, teaches men, punishes men, forgives men, saves men from their sins; and Him I have found in the Bible, and nowhere else, save in the facts of life which the Bible alone interprets.

In the power of man to find out God I will never believe. The 'religious sentiment,' or 'God-consciousness,' so much talked of now-a-days, seems to me (as I believe it will to all practical common-sense Englishmen), a faculty not to be depended on; as fallible and corrupt as any other part of human nature; apt (to judge from history) to develop itself into ugly forms, not only without a revelation from God, but too often in spite of one—into polytheisms, idolatries, witchcrafts, Buddhist asceticisms, Phœnician Moloch-sacrifices, Popish inquisitions, American spirit-rappings, and what not. The hearts and minds of the sick, the poor, the sorrowing, the truly human, all demand a living God, who has revealed himself in living acts; a God who has taught mankind by facts, not left them to discover him by theories and sentiments; a Judge, a Father, a Saviour, and an Inspirer; in a word, their hearts and minds demand the historic truth of the Bible—of the Old Testament no less than of the New.

What I needed therefore, for my guidance, was a book which should believe and confess all this, without condemning or ignoring free criticism and its results; which should make use of that criticism not to destroy but to build up; which employed a thorough knowledge of the Old Testament history, the manners of the Jews, the localities of the sacred events, to teach men not what might not be in the Bible, but what was certainly therein ; which dealt with the Bible after the only fair and trustful method ; that is, to consider it at first according to the theory which it sets forth concerning itself, before trying quite another theory of the commentator's own invention ; and which combined with a courageous determination to tell the truth, the whole truth, and nothing but the truth, that Christian spirit of trust, reverence and piety, without which all intellectual acuteness is but blindness and folly.

All this, and more, I found in your book, enforced with a genius which needs no poor praise of mine ; and I hailed its appearance at such a crisis as a happy Providence, certain that it would be, what I now know by experience it has been, a balm to many a wounded spirit, and a check to many a wandering intellect, inclined, in the rashness of youth, to throw away the truth it already had, for the sake of theories which it hoped that it might possibly verify hereafter.

With your book in my hand, I have tried to write a few plain Sermons, telling plain people what they will find in the Pentateuch, in spite of all present doubts, as their fathers found it before them, and as (I trust) their children will find it after them, when all this present whirlwind of controversy has past,

> 'As dust that lightly rises up,
> And is lightly laid again.'

I have told them that they will find in the Bible, and in no other ancient book, that living working God, whom their reason and conscience demand ; and that they will find that he is none other than Jesus Christ our Lord. I have not apologised for or explained away the so-called 'Anthropomorphism' of the Old Testament. On the contrary, I have frankly accepted it, and even gloried in it as an integral, and I believe invaluable element of Scripture. I have deliberately ignored many questions of great interest and difficulty, because I had no satisfactory solution of them to offer ; but I have said at the same time that those questions were altogether unimportant, compared with those salient and fundamental points of the Bible history on which I was preaching. And therefore I have dared to bid my people relinquish Biblical criticism to those who have time for it; and to say of it with me, as Abraham of the planets, 'O my people, I am clear of all these things! I turn myself to him who made heaven and earth.'

I do not wish, believe me, to make you responsible for any statement or opinion of mine. I am painfully conscious, on reviewing for the Press Sermons which would never have been published save by special request, how imperfect, poor, and weak they seem to me—how much worse, then, they will appear to other people; how much more may be said which I have not the wit to say ! But the Bible can take care of itself, I presume, without my help. All I can do is, to speak what I think, as far as I see my way ; to record the obligation toward you under which I, with thousands more, now lie; and to express my hope that we shall be always found together fellow-workers in the cause of Truth, and that to you and in you may be fulfilled those noble and tender words, in which you have spoken of Samuel, and of those who work in Samuel's spirit:

'In later times, even in our own, many names spring to our recollection of those who have trodden or (in different degrees, some known, and some unknown) are treading the same thankless path in the Church of Germany, in the Church of France, in the Church of Russia, in the Church of England. Wherever they are, and whosoever they may be, and howsoever they may be neglected, or assailed, or despised, they, like their great prototype and likeness in the Jewish Church, are the silent healers who bind up the wounds of their age in spite of itself; they are the good physicians who bind together the dislocated bones of a disjointed time; they are the reconcilers who turn the hearts of the children to the fathers, or of the fathers to the children. They have but little praise and reward from the partisans who are loud in indiscriminate censure and applause. But, like Samuel, they have a far higher reward, in the Davids who are silently strengthened and nurtured by them in Naioth of Ramah—in the glories of a new age which shall be ushered in peacefully and happily after they have been laid in the grave.'*

That such, my dear Stanley, may be your work and your destiny, is the earnest hope of

Yours affectionately,
C. KINGSLEY.

Eversley Rectory,
July 1, 1863.

---

* *Lectures on the Jewish Church*, Lect. xviii. p. 401.

SERMON I.

GOD IN CHRIST.

(Septuagesima Sunday.)

GENESIS i. 1.

In the beginning God created the heaven and the earth.

WE have begun this Sunday to read the book of Genesis. I trust that you will listen to it as you ought—with peculiar respect and awe, as the oldest part of the Bible, and therefore the oldest of all known works—the earliest human thought which has been handed down to us.

And what is the first written thought which has been handed down to us by the Providence of Almighty God?

'In the beginning God created the heaven and the earth.'

How many other things, how many hundred other things, men might have thought fit to write down for those who should come after; and say—

1.

This is the first knowledge which a man should have; this is the root of all wisdom, all power, all wealth.

But God inspired Moses and the Prophets to write as they have written. They were not to tell men that the first thing to be learnt was how to be rich; nor how to be strong; nor even how to be happy: but that the first thing to be learnt was that God created the heaven and the earth.

And why first?

Because the first question which man asks—the question which shows he is a man and not a brute—always has been, and always will be—Where am I? How did I get into this world; and how did this world get here likewise? And if man takes up with a wrong answer to that question, then the man himself is certain to go wrong, in all manner of ways. For a lie can never do anything but harm, or breed anything but harm; and lies do breed, as fast as the blight on the trees, or the smut on the corn: only being not according to nature, or the laws of God, they do not breed as natural things do, after their kind: but, belonging to chaos, the kingdom of disorder and misrule, they breed fresh lies unlike themselves, of all strange and unexpected shapes; so

that when a man takes up with one lie, there is
no saying what other lie he may not take up with
beside.

Wherefore the first thing man has to learn is
truth concerning the first human question, Where
am I? How did I come here; and how did this
world come here? To which the Bible answers
in its first line—

'In the beginning God created the heaven and
the earth.'

How God created, the Bible does not tell us.
Whether he created (as doubtless he could have
done if he chose) this world suddenly out of nothing, full grown and complete; or whether he
created it (as he creates you and me, and all living
and growing things now) out of things which had
been before it—that the Bible does not tell us.

Perhaps if it had told us, it would have drawn
away our minds to think of natural things, and
what we now call science, instead of keeping our
minds fixed, as it now does, on spiritual things,
and above all on the Spirit of all spirits; Him of
whom it is written, 'God is a Spirit.'

For the Bible is simply the revelation, or unveiling of God. It is not a book of natural
science. It is not merely a book of holy and

virtuous precepts. It is not merely a book wherein we may find a scheme of salvation for our souls. It is a book of the revelation, or unveiling of the Lord God, Jesus Christ ; what he was, what he is, and what he will be for ever.

Of Jesus Christ? How is he revealed in the text, 'In the beginning God created the heaven and the earth ?'

Thus :—If you look at the first chapter of Genesis and the beginning of the second, you will see that God is called therein by a different name from what he is called afterwards. He is called God, Elohim, The High or Mighty One or Ones. After that he is called the Lord God, Jehovah Elohim, which means properly, The High or Mighty I Am, or Jehovah, a word which I will explain to you afterwards. That word is generally translated in our Bible, as it was in the Greek, 'The Lord ;' because the later Jews had such a deep reverence for the name of Jehovah, that they did not like to write it or speak it : but called God simply Adonai, the Lord.

So that we have three names for God in the Old Testament.

First El, or Elohim, the Mighty One : by which, so Moses says, God was known to the Jews before his time, and which sets forth God's power and majesty—the first thing of which men would think in thinking of God.

Next Jehovah. The I Am, the Eternal, and Self-existent Being, by which name God revealed himself to Moses in the burning bush—a deeper and wider name than the former.

And lastly, Adonai, the Lord, the living Ruler and Master of the world and men, by which he revealed himself to the later Jews, and at last to all mankind in the person of our Lord Jesus Christ.

Now I need not to trouble your mind or my own with arguments as to how these three different names got into the Bible.

That is a matter of criticism, of scholarship, with which you have nothing to do: and you may thank God that you have not, in such days as these. Your business is, not how the names got there, which is a matter of criticism, but why they have been left there by the providence of God, which is a matter of simple religion; and you may thank God, I say again, that it is so. For scholarship is Martha's part, which must be done, and yet which cumbers a man with much serving: but simple heart religion is the better part which Mary chose; and of which the Lord has said, that it shall not be taken from her, nor from those who, like her, sit humbly at the feet of the Lord, and hear his voice, without troubling their souls with questions of words, and endless genealogies, which eat out the hearts of men.

Therefore all I shall say about the matter is, that the first chapter of Genesis, and the first three verses of the second, may be the writing of a prophet older than Moses, because they call God Elohim, which was his name before Moses' time; and that Moses may have used them, and worked them into a book of Genesis; while he, in the part which he wrote himself, called God at first by the name Jehovah Elohim, The Lord God, in order to show that Jehovah and El were the same God, and not two different ones; and after he had made the Jews understand that, went on to call God simply Jehovah, and to use the two names, as they are used through the rest of the Old Testament, interchangeably: as we say some- times God, sometimes the Lord, sometimes the Deity, and so forth; meaning of course always the same Being.

That, I think, is the probable and simple account which tallies most exactly with the Bible.

As for the first five books of the Bible, the Pentateuch, having been written by Moses, or at least by far the greater part of them, I cannot see the least reason to doubt it.

The Bible itself does not say so; and therefore it is not a matter of faith, and men may have their own opinions on the matter, without sin or false doctrine. But that Moses wrote part at least of them, our Lord and his Apostles say expressly. The tradition of the Jews (who really ought to know best) has always been that Moses wrote either the whole or the greater part. Moses is by far the most likely man to have written them, of all of whom we read in Scripture. We have not the least proof, and, what is more, never shall or can have, that he did not write them. And therefore, I advise you to believe, as I do, that the universal tradition of both Jews and Christians is right, when it calls these books, the books of Moses.*

---

* I must say that all attempts to put a later date on these books seems to me to fail simply from want of evidence. I must say, also, that all attempts to distinguish between 'Jehovistic' and 'Elohistic' documents (with the exception, perhaps, of the first chapter of Genesis) seem to me to fail likewise; and that the theory of an Elohistic and a Jehovistic sect has received its *reductionem ad absurdum* in a certain recent criticism of the Psalms.

But now no more of these matters: we will think of a matter quite infinitely more important, and that is, *Who* is this God whom the Bible reveals to us, from the very first verse of Genesis?

At least, he is one and the same Being. Whether he be called El, Jehovah, or Adonai, he is the same Lord.

It is the Lord who makes the heaven and the earth, the Lord who puts man in a Paradise, lays on him a commandment, and appears to him in visible shape.

It is the Lord who speaks to Abraham: though Abraham knew him only as El-Shaddai, the Almighty God. It is the Lord who brings the Israelites out of Egypt, who gives them the law on Sinai. It is the Lord who speaks to Samuel, to David, to all the Prophets, and appears to Isaiah, while his glory fills the Temple. In whatever 'divers manners' and 'many portions,' as St. Paul says in the Epistle to the Hebrews, he speaks to them, he is the same Being.

And Psalmists and Prophets are most careful to tell us that he is the God, not of the Jews only, but of the Gentiles; of all mankind—as indeed, he must be, being Jehovah, the I Am, the one Self-existent and Eternal Being; that from his throne he is watching and judging all the nations upon earth, fashioning the hearts of all, appointing them their bounds, and the times of their habitation, if haply they may seek after him and find him, though he be not far from any one of them; for in him they live and move and have their being.

This is the message of Moses, of the Psalmists and the Prophets, just as much as of St. Paul on Mars' Hill at Athens.

So begins and so ends the Old Testament, revealing throughout The Lord.

And how does the New Testament begin?

By telling us that a Babe was born at Bethlehem, and called Jesus, the Saviour.

But who is this blessed Babe? He, too, is The Lord.

'A Saviour, which is Christ the Lord.' And from thence, through the Gospels, the Acts, the Epistles, the Revelation of St. John, he is the Lord. There is no manner of doubt of it. The Apostles and Evangelists take no trouble to prove it. They take it for granted. They call Jesus Christ by the name by which the Jews had for hundreds of years called the El of Abraham, the Jehovah of Moses. The Babe who is born at Bethlehem, who grows up as other human beings grow, into the man Christ Jesus, is none other than the Lord God who created the universe, who made a covenant with Abraham, who brought the Israelites out of Egypt, who inspired the Prophets, who has been from the beginning governing all the earth.

It is very awful. But you must believe that, or put your Bibles away as a dream—New Testament and Old alike. Not to believe that fully and utterly, is not to believe the Bible at all. For that is what the Bible says, and has been sent into the world to say. It is, from beginning to end, the book of the revelation, or unveiling of Jesus Christ, very God of very God.

But some may say, 'Why tell us that? Of course we believe it. We should not be Christians if we did not.'

Be it so. I hope it is so. But I think that it is not so easy to believe it as we fancy.

We believe it, I think, more firmly than our forefathers did five hundred years ago, on some points; and therefore we have got rid of many dark and blasphemous superstitions about witches and devils, about the evil of the earth and of our own bodies, of marriage, and of the common duties and bonds of humanity, which tormented them, because they could not believe fully that Jesus Christ had created, and still ruled the world and all therein.

But we are all too apt still to think of Jesus Christ merely as some one who can save our souls when we die, and to forget that he is the Lord, who is and has been always ruling the world and all mankind.

And from this come two bad consequences. People are apt to speak of the Lord Jesus—or at least to admire preachers who speak of him—as if he belonged to them, and not they to him; and, therefore, to speak of him with an irreverence and a familiarity which they dared not use, if they really believed that this same Jesus, whose name they take in vain, is none other than the Living God himself, their Creator, by whom every blade of grass grows beneath their feet, every planet and star rolls above their heads.

And next—they fancy that the Old Testament speaks of our Lord Jesus Christ only in a few mysterious prophecies—some of which there is reason to suspect they quite misinterpret. They are slow of heart to believe all that the Scriptures have spoken of him of whom Moses and the

Prophets did write, not in a few scattered texts, but in every line of the Old Testament, from the first of Genesis to the last of Malachi.

And therefore they believe less and less, that Jesus Christ is still the Lord in any real practical sense—not merely the Lord of a few elect or saints, but the Lord of man and of the earth, and of the whole universe. They think of him as a Lord who will come again to judgment—which is true, and awfully true, in the very deepest sense: but they do not think of him—in spite of what he himself and his apostles declared of him —as The Living, Working Lord, to whom all power is given in heaven and earth, and not merely over the souls of a few regenerate; as the Alpha and Omega, the first and the last, of whom St. Paul says, 'that the mystery of Christ has been hid from the beginning of the world in God, who created all things by Jesus Christ.' * * * 'That, in the dispensation of the fulness of times, he might gather together in one all things in Christ, both which are in heaven, and which are in earth.' They fill their minds with fancies about the book of Revelation, most of which, there is reason to fear, are little else but fancies: while they overlook what that book really does say, and what is the best news that the world ever heard, that he is the Prince of the kings of the earth.

Therefore they have fears for Christ's Bible, fears for Christ's Church, fears for the fate of the world, which they could not have if they would recollect who Christ is, and believe that he is able to take care of his own kingdom and power and glory, better than man can take care of it for him. Surely, surely, faith in the living Lord who rules the world in righteousness is fast dying out among us; and many who call themselves Christians seem to know less of Christ, and of the work which he is carrying on in the world, than did the old Psalmist, who said of him, 'The Lord shall endure for ever; he hath also prepared his seat for judgment. For he shall judge the world in righteousness, and minister true judgment among the people.' He fashioneth 'the hearts of all of them, and understandeth all their works.'

Who can say that he believes that, who holds that this world is the devil's world, and that sinful man and evil spirits are having it all their own way till the day of judgment?

Who can say that he believes that, who falls into pitiable terror at every new discovery of science or of scholarship, for fear it should destroy the Bible and the Christian faith, instead of believing that all which makes manifest is light, and that all light comes from the Father of lights, by the providence of Jesus Christ his only-begotten Son, who is the light of men, and the inspiration of his Spirit, who leadeth into all truth?

And how, lastly, can those say that they believe that, who will lie, and slander, and have recourse to base intrigues, in order to defend that truth, and that Church, of which the Lord himself has said that he has founded it upon a rock, and the gates of hell shall not prevail against it?

But if you believe indeed the message of the Bible, that Jesus Christ is the Lord who made heaven and earth, then it shall be said of you, as it was of St. Peter, 'Blessed art thou: for flesh and blood hath not revealed it to thee, but my Father which is in heaven.'

Yes. Blessed indeed is he who believes that; who believes that the same person who was born in a stable, had not where to lay his head, went about healing the sick and binding up the broken heart, suffered under Pontius Pilate, was crucified, dead, and buried, and rose again the third day, and ascended into heaven—ascended thither that he might fill all things; and if none other than the

Lord of the earth and of men, the Creator, the Teacher, the Saviour, the Guide, the King, the Judge, of all the world, and of all worlds past, present, and to come.

For to him who thus believes shall be fulfilled the promise of his Lord, 'Come unto me, all ye that are weary and heavy laden, and I will give you rest.'

He will find rest unto his soul. Rest from that first and last question, of which I said that all men, down to the lowest savage, ask it, simply because they are men, and not beasts. Where am I? How came I here? How came this world here likewise?

For he can answer—

'I am in the kingdom of the Babe of Bethlehem. He put me here. And he put this world here likewise: and that is enough for me. He created all I see or can see—I care little how, provided that HE created it; for then I am sure that it must be very good. He redeemed me and all mankind, when we were lost, at the price of his most precious blood. He the Lord is King, therefore will I not be moved, though the earth be shaken, and the hills be carried into the midst of the sea. Yea, though the sun were turned to darkness, and the moon to blood, and the stars fell from heaven, and all power and order, all belief and custom of mankind, were turned upside down, yet there would still be One above who rules the world in righteousness, whose eye is on them that fear him and put their trust in his mercy, to deliver their soul from death, and to feed them in the time of dearth. Darkness may cover the land for awhile, and gross darkness the people. But while I sit in darkness, the Lord shall be my light, till the day when he shall say once more, "Let there be light," and light shall be.'

Yes. To the man who is a good man and true; who has any hearty Christian feeling for his fellow-men, and is not merely a selfish superstitious person, caring for nothing but what he calls the safety of his own soul; to the man, I say, who has anything of the loving spirit of Christ in him, what question can be more important than this, Is the world well made or ill? Is it well governed or ill? Is it on the whole going right or going wrong? And what can be more comforting to such a man, than the answer which the Bible gives at the outset?—

This world is well made, in love and care; for Christ the Lord made it, and behold it was very good.

This world is going right and not wrong, in spite of all appearances to the contrary; for Christ the Lord is King. He sitteth between the cherubim, be the earth never so unquiet. He is too strong and too loving to let the world go any way but the right. Parts of it will often go wrong here, and go wrong there. The sin and ignorance of men will disturb his order, and rebel against his laws; and strange and mad things, terrible and pitiable things will happen, as they have happened ever since the day when the first man disobeyed the commandment of the Lord. But man cannot conquer the Lord; the Lord will conquer man. He will teach men by their neighbours' sins. He will teach them by their own sins. He will chastise them by sore judgments. He will make fearful examples of wilful and conceited sinners; and those who seem to escape him in this life, shall not escape him in the life to come. But he is trying for ever every man's work by fire; and against that fire no lie will stand. He will burn up the stubble and chaff, and leave only the pure wheat for the use of future generations. His purpose will stand. His word will never return to him void, but will prosper always where he sends it. He has made the round world so sure that it cannot be moved, either by man or by worse than man. His ever-lasting laws will take effect in spite of all opposition, and bring the world and man along the path, and to the end, which he purposed for them in the day when God made the heavens and the earth, and in that even greater day, when he said, 'Let us make man in our image, after our likeness,' and man arose upright, and knew that he was not as the beasts, and asked who he was, and where? feeling with the hardly opened eyes of his spirit after that Lord from whom he came, and to whom he shall return, as many as have eternal life, in the day when Christ the Lord of life shall have destroyed death, and put all enemies under his feet, and given up the king-dom to God, even the Father, that God may be all in all.

SERMON II.

THE LIKENESS OF GOD.

(Trinity Sunday.)

GENESIS i. 26.

And God said, Let us make man in our image, after our
likeness.

THIS is a hard saying. It is difficult at times to believe it to be true.

If one looks not at what God has made man, but at what man has made himself, one will never believe it to be true.

When one looks at what man has made himself; at the back streets of some of our great cities; at the thousands of poor Germans and Irish across the ocean bribed to kill and to be killed, they know not why; at the abominable wrongs and cruelties going on in Poland at this moment—the cry whereof is going up to the ears of the God of Hosts, and surely not in vain; when one thinks of all the cries which have gone up in all ages from the victims of man's greed, lust, cruelty, tyranny, and shrillest of all from the tortured victims of his superstition and fanaticism, it is difficult to answer the sneer, 'Believe, if you can, that this foolish, unjust, cruel being called man, is made in the likeness of God. Man was never made in the image of God at all. He is only a cunninger sort of animal, for better for worse— and for worse as often as for better.'

Another says, not quite that. Man was in the likeness of God once, but he lost that by Adam's fall, and now is only an animal with an immortal soul in him, to be lost or saved.

There is more truth in that latter notion than in the former: but if it be quite right; if we did lose the likeness of God at Adam's fall, how comes the Bible never to say so? How comes the Bible never to say one word on what must have been the most important thing which ever happened to mankind before the coming of our Lord Jesus Christ?

And how comes it also that the New Testament says distinctly that man is still made in the likeness of God? For St. Paul speaks of man as 'the likeness and glory of God.' And St. James says of the tongue, 'Therewith bless we God, even the Father; and therewith' (to our shame) 'curse we men, which are made in the likeness of God.'

But the great proof that man is made in the image and likeness of God is the incarnation of our Lord Jesus Christ; for if human nature had been, as some think, something utterly brutish and devilish, and utterly unlike God, how could God have become man without ceasing to be God? Christ was man of the substance of his mother. That substance had the same human nature as we have. Then if that human nature be evil, what follows? Something which I shall not utter, for it is blasphemy. Christ has taken the manhood into God. Then if manhood be evil, what follows again? Something more which I shall not utter, for it is blasphemy.

But man is made in the image of God; and therefore God, in whose image he is made, could take on himself his own image and likeness, and become perfect man, without ceasing to be perfect God.

Therefore, my friends, it is a comfortable and wholesome doctrine, that man is made in the image of God, and one for which we must thank the Bible. For it is the Bible which has revealed that truth to us, in its very beginning and outset, that we might have, from the first, clear and sound notions concerning man and God. The Bible, I say; for the sacred books of the heathen say, most of them, nothing thereof.

Man has, in all ages, been tempted, when he looks at his own wickedness and folly, not only to despise himself—which he has good reason enough to do—but to despise his own human nature, and to cry to God, 'Why hast thou made me thus?' He has cursed his own human nature. He has said, 'Surely man is most miserable of all the beasts of the field.' He has said, 'I must get rid of my human nature—I must give up wife, family, human life of all kinds, I must go into the deserts and the forests, and there try to forget that I am a man, and become a mere spirit or angel.' So said the Buddhists of Asia, the deepest thinkers concerning man and God of all the heathens, and so have many said since their time. But so does the Bible not say. It starts by telling us that man is made in God's likeness, and that therefore his human nature is originally and in itself not a bad, but a perfectly good thing. All that has to be done to it is to be cured of its diseases; and the Bible declares that it can be cured. Howsoever man may have fallen, he may rise. Howsoever the likeness may be blotted and corrupted, it can be cleansed and renewed. Howsoever it may be perverted and turned right round and away from God and goodness to selfishness and evil, it can be converted, and turned back again to God. Howsoever utterly far gone man may be from original righteousness, still to original righteousness he can return, by the grace of baptism and the renewing of the Holy Spirit.

And what in us is the likeness of God? That is a deep question.

Only one answer will I make to it to-day. Whatever in us is, or is not, the likeness of God, at least the sense of right and wrong is; to know right and wrong. So says the Bible itself, 'Behold the man is become as one of us, to know good and evil.' Not that he got the likeness of God by his fall—of course not; but that he became aware of his likeness, and that in a very painful and common way—by sinning against it; as St. Paul says in one of his deepest utterances, 'By sin is the knowledge of the law.'

And you may see for yourselves how human nature can have God's likeness in that respect, and yet be utterly fallen and corrupt.

For a man may—and indeed every man does —know good and yet be unable to do it, and know evil, and yet be a slave to it, tied and bound with the chains of his sins till the grace of God release him from them.

To know good and evil, right and wrong—to have a conscience, a moral sense—that is the likeness of God of which I wish to preach to-day. Because it is through *that* knowledge of good and evil, and through it alone, that we can know God, and Jesus Christ whom he has sent. It is through our moral sense that God speaks to us; through our sense of right and wrong; through that I say, God speaks to us, whether in reproof or encouragement, in wrath or in love; to teach us what he is like, and to teach us what he is not like.

To know God. That is the side on which we must look at this text on Trinity Sunday. If man be made in the image of God, then we may be able to know something at least of God, and of the character of God. If we have the copy, we can guess at least at what the original is like.

From the character, therefore, of every good man, we may guess at something of the character of God. But from the character of Jesus Christ our Lord, who is the very brightness of his Father's glory and the express image of his person, we may see perfectly—at least perfectly enough for all our needs in this life, and in the life to come—what is the character of God, who made heaven and earth.

I beseech you to remember this—I beseech you to believe this, with your whole hearts, and minds, and souls, and especially just now.

For there are many abroad now who will tell you, man can know nothing of God.

Answer them: 'If your God be a God of whom I can know nothing, then he is not my God, the God of the Bible. For he is the God who has said of old, "They shall not teach each man his brother, saying, Know the Lord, for all shall know Me, from the least unto the greatest." He is the God, who, through Jesus Christ our Lord, accused and blamed the Jews because they did *not* know him, which if they *could not* know him would have been no fault of theirs. Of doctrines, and notions, and systems, it is written, and most truly, "I know in part, and I prophesy in part," and again, "If a man thinketh that he knoweth anything, he knoweth nothing yet as he ought to know." But of God it is written, "This is life eternal, to know thee, the only true God, and Jesus Christ, whom thou hast sent." '

But they will say, man is finite and limited, God is infinite and absolute, and how can the finite comprehend the infinite?

Answer: 'Those are fine words: I do not understand them; and I do not care to understand them; I do not deny that God is infinite and absolute, though what that means I do not know. But I find nothing about his being infinite and absolute in the Bible. I find there that he is righteous, just, loving, merciful, and forgiving; and that he is angry too, and that his wrath is a consuming fire, and I know well enough what those words mean, though I do not know what infinite and absolute mean. So that is what I have to think of, for my own sake and the sake of all mankind.'

But, they will say, you must not take these words to the letter; man is so unlike God, and God so unlike man, that God's attributes must be quite different from man's. When you read of God's love, justice, anger, and so forth, you must not think that they are anything like man's love, man's justice, man's anger; but something quite different, not only in degree, but in kind:

so that what might be unjust and cruel in man, would not be so in God.

My dear friends, beware of that doctrine; for out of it have sprung half the fanaticism and superstition which has disgraced and tormented the earth. Beware of ever thinking that a wrong thing would be right if God did it, and not you. And mind, that is flatly contrary to the letter of the Bible. In that grand text where Abraham pleads with God, what does he say? Not, 'Of course if Thou choosest to do it, it must be right,' but 'Shall not the Judge of all the earth do RIGHT?' Abraham actually refers the Almighty God to his own law; and asserts an eternal rule of right and wrong common to man and to God, which God will surely never break.

Answer: 'If that doctrine be true, which I will never believe, then the Bible mocks and deceives poor miserable sinful man, instead of teaching him. If God's love does not mean real actual love,—God's anger, actual anger,—God's forgiveness, real forgiveness,—God's justice, real justice,—God's truth, real truth,—God's faithfulness, real faithfulness, what do they mean? Nothing which I can understand, nothing which I can trust in. How can I trust in a God whom I cannot understand or know? How can I trust in a love or a justice which is not what *I* call love or justice, or anything like them?

'The saints of old said, *I know* in whom I have believed. And how can I believe in him, if there is nothing in him which I can know; nothing which is like man—nothing, to speak plainly, like Christ, who was perfect man as well as perfect God? If that be so, if man can know nothing really of God, he is indeed most miserable of all the beasts of the field, for I will warrant that he can know nothing really of anything else. And what is left for him, but to remain for this life, and the life to come, in the outer darkness of ignorance and confusion, misrule and misery, wherein is most literally—as one may see in the history of every heathen nation upon earth — wailing and gnashing of teeth.

'If God's goodness be not like man's goodness, there is no rule of morality left, no eternal standard of right and wrong. How can I tell what I ought to do; or what God expects of me; or when I am right and when I am wrong, if you take from me the good, plain, old Bible rule, that man *can* be, and *must* be, like God? The Bible rule is, that everything good in man must be exactly like something good in God, because it is inspired into him by the Spirit of God himself. Our Lord Jesus, who spoke, not to philosophers or Scribes and Pharisees, but to plain human beings, weeping and sorrowing, suffering and sinning, like us,—told them to be perfect, as our Father in heaven is perfect, by being good to the unthankful and the evil. And if man is to be perfect, as his Father in heaven is perfect, then his Father in heaven is perfect as man ought to be perfect. He told us to be merciful as our Father in heaven is merciful. Then our Father in heaven is merciful with the same sort of mercy as we ought to show. We are bidden to forgive others, even as God for Christ's sake has forgiven us: then if our forgiveness is to be like God's, God's forgiveness is like ours. We are to be true, because God is true: just, because God is just. How can we be that, if God's truth is not like what men call truth, God's justice not like what men call justice?

'If I give up that rule of right and wrong, I give up all rules of right and wrong whatsoever.'

No, my friends; if we will seek for God where he may be found, then we shall know God, whom truly to know is everlasting life. But we must not seek for him where he is not, in long words and notions of philosophy spun out of men's brains, and set up as if they were real things, when words and notions they are, and words and notions they will remain. We must look for God where he is to be found, in the character of his only begotten Son, Jesus Christ, who alone has revealed and unveiled God's character, because he is the brightness of God's glory, and the express image of his person.

What Christ's character was we can find in the Holy Gospels; and we can find it too, scattered and in parts, in all the good, the holy, the noble, who have aught of Christ's spirit and likeness in them.

Whatsoever is good and beautiful in any human soul, that is the likeness of Christ. Whatsoever thoughts, words, or deeds are true, honest, just, pure, lovely, of good report; whatsoever is true virtue, whatsoever is truly worthy of praise, that is the likeness of Christ; the likeness of him who was full of all purity, all tenderness, all mercy, all self-sacrifice, all benevolence, all helpfulness; full of all just and noble indignation also against oppressors and hypocrites who bound heavy burdens and grievous to be borne, but touched them not themselves with one of their fingers; who kept the key of knowledge, and neither entered in themselves, or let those who were trying enter in either.

The likeness of an all-noble, all-just, all-gracious, all-wise, all-good human being; that is the likeness of Christ, and that, therefore, is the likeness of God who made heaven and earth.

All-good; utterly and perfectly good, in every kind of goodness which we have ever seen, or can ever imagine—that, thank God, is the likeness and character of Almighty God, in whom we live and move, and have our being. To know that he is that—all-good, is to know his character as far as sinful and sorrowful man need know; and is not that to know enough?

The mystery of the ever-blessed Trinity, as set forth so admirably in the Athanasian Creed, is a mystery; and it we cannot *know*—we can only believe it, and take it on trust: but the *character* of the ever-blessed Trinity—Father, Son, and Holy Ghost—we can know: while by keeping the words of the Athanasian Creed carefully in mind, we may be kept from many grievous and hurtful mistakes which will hinder our knowing it. We can know that they are all good, for such as the Father is such is the Son, and such is the Holy Ghost. That goodness is their one and eternal substance, and majesty, and glory, which we must not divide by fancying with some, that the Father is good in one way and the Son in another. That their goodness is eternal and unchangeable; for they themselves are eternal, and have neither parts nor passions. That their goodness is incomprehensible, that is, cannot be bounded or limited by time or space, or by any notions or doctrines of ours, for they themselves are incomprehensible, and able to do abundantly more than we can ask or think.

This is our God, the God of the Bible, the God of the Church, the God who has revealed himself in Jesus Christ our Lord. And him we can believe utterly, for we know that he is faithful and true; and we know what *that* means, if there is any truth or faithfulness in us. We know that he is just and righteous; and we know what *that* means, if there is any justice and uprightness in ourselves. Him we can trust utterly; to him we can take all our cares, all our sorrows, all our doubts, all our sins, and pour them out to him, because he is condescending; and we know what *that* means, if there be any condescension and real high-mindedness in ourselves. We can be certain too that he will hear us, just because he is so great, so majestic, so glorious; because his greatness, and majesty, and glory is a moral and spiritual greatness, which shows itself by stooping to the meanest, by listening to the most foolish, helping the weakest, pitying the worst, even while it is bound to punish. Him we can trust, I say, because him we can know, and can say of him, Let the Infinite and the Absolute mean what they may, I know in whom I have believed—God the Good. Whatever else I cannot understand, I can at least 'understand the lovingkindness of the Lord;' however high his dwelling may be, I know that he humbleth himself to behold the things in heaven and earth, to take the simple out of the dust, and the poor out of the mire. Whatever else God may or may not be, I know that gracious is the Lord, and righteous, yea, our God is merciful. The Lord preserveth the simple, for *I* was in misery, and he helped *me*. Whatsoever fine theories or new discoveries I cannot trust, I can trust him, for with him is mercy, and with the Lord is plenteous redemption; and he shall redeem his people from all their sins. However dark and ignorant I may be, I can go to him for teaching, and say, Teach me to do the thing that pleaseth thee, for thou art my God; let thy loving Spirit lead me forth into the land of righteousness.

The land of righteousness. The one true heavenly land, wherein God the righteous dwelleth from eternity to eternity, righteous in all his ways, and holy in all his works, and therefore adorable in all his ways, and glorious in all his works, with a glory even greater than the glory of his Almighty power. On that glory of his goodness we can gaze, though afar off in degree, yet near in kind, while the glory of his wisdom and power is far, far beyond my understanding. Of the intellect of God we can know nothing; but we can know what is better, the heart of God. For *that* glory of goodness we can understand, and *know*, and sympathize with in our heart of hearts, and say, If *this* be the likeness of God, he is indeed worthy to be worshipped, and had in honour. Praise the Lord, O my soul, for the Lord is *good.* Kings and all people, princes and all judges of the world, young men and maidens, old men and children, praise the name of the Lord, for his name only is excellent, because his name is *good.*

Lift up your eyes, and look upon the face of Christ the God-man, crucified for you; and behold therein the truth of all truths, the doctrine of all doctrines, the gospel of all gospels, that the 'Unknown,' and 'Infinite,' and 'Absolute' God, who made the universe, bids you know him, and know this of him, that he is *good*, and that his express image and likeness is—Jesus Christ, his Son, our Lord.

SERMON III.

THE VOICE OF THE LORD GOD.

(Preached also at the Chapel Royal, St. James'. Sexagesima Sunday.)

GENESIS iii. 8.

And they heard the voice of the Lord God walking in the garden in the cool of the day.

THESE words would startle us, if we heard them for the first time. I do not know but that they may startle us now, often as we have heard them, if we think seriously over them. That God should appear to mortal man, and speak with mortal man. It is most wonderful. It is utterly unlike anything that we have ever seen, or that any person on earth has seen, for many hundred years. It is a miracle, in every sense of the word.

When one compares man as he was then, weak and ignorant, and yet seemingly so favoured by God, so near to God, with man as he is now, strong and cunning, spreading over the earth and replenishing it; subduing it with railroads and steamships, with agriculture and science, and all strange and crafty inventions, and all the while never visited by any Divine or heavenly appearance, but seemingly left utterly to himself by God, to go his own way and do his own will upon the earth, one asks with wonder, Can we be Adam's children? Can the God who appeared to Adam, be our God likewise, or has God's plan and rule for teaching man changed utterly?

No. He is one God; the same God yesterday, to-day, and for ever. His will and purpose, his care and rule over man, have not changed.

That is a matter of faith. Of the faith which the holy Church commands us to have. But it need not be a blind or unreasonable faith. That our God is the God of Adam; that the same Lord God who taught him teaches us likewise, need not be a mere matter of faith: it may be a matter of reason likewise; a thing which seems reasonable to us, and recommends itself to our mind and conscience as true.

Consider, my friends, a babe when it comes into the world. The first thing of which it is aware is its mother's bosom. The first thing which it does, as its eyes and ears are gradually opened to this world, is to cling to its parents. It holds fast by their hand, it will not leave their side. It is afraid to sleep alone, to go alone. To them it looks up for food and help. Of them it asks questions, and tries to learn from them, to copy them, to do what it sees them doing, even in play; and the parents in return lavish care and tenderness on it, and will not let it out of their sight. But after a while, as the child grows, the parents will not let it be so perpetually with them. It must go to school. It must see its parents only very seldom, perhaps it must be away from them weeks or months. And why? Not that the parents love it less : but that it must learn to take care of itself, to act for itself, to think for itself, or it will never grow up to be a rational human being.

And the parting of the child from the parents does not break the bond of love between them. It learns to love them even better. Neither does it break the bond of obedience. The child is away from its parents' eye. But it learns to obey them behind their back; to do their will of its own will; to ask itself, What would my parents wish me to do, were they here? and so learns, if it will think of it, a more true, deep, honourable and spiritual obedience, than it ever would, if its parents were perpetually standing over it, saying, Do this, and do that.

In after life, that child may settle far away from his father's home. He may go up into the temptations and bustle of some great city. He may cross to far lands beyond the sea. But need he love his parents less? need the bond between them be broken, though he may never set eyes on them again? God forbid. He may be settled far away, with children, business, interests of his own; and yet he may be doing all the while his father's will. The lessons of God which he learnt at his mother's knee may be still a lamp to his feet and a light to his path. Amid all the bustle and labour of business, his father's face may still be before his eyes, his father's voice still sound in his ears, bidding him be a worthy son to him still; bidding him not to leave that way wherein he should go, in which his parents trained him long, long since. He may feel that his parents are near him in the spirit, though absent in the flesh. Yes, though they may have passed altogether out of this world, they may be to him present and near at hand; and he may be kept from doing many a wrong thing and encouraged to do many a right one, by the ennobling thought, My father would have had it so, my mother would have had it so, had they been here on earth. And though in this world he may never see them again, he may look forward steadily and longingly to the day when, this life's battle over, he shall meet again in heaven those who gave him life on earth.

My friends, if this be the education which is natural and necessary from our earthly parents, made in God's image, appointed by God's eternal laws for each of us, why should it not be the education which God himself has appointed for mankind? All which is truly human (not sinful or fallen) is an image and pattern of something Divine. May not therefore the training which we find, by the very facts of nature, fit and necessary for our children, be the same as God's training, by which he fashioneth the hearts of the children of men? Therefore we can believe the Bible when it tells us that so it is. That God began the education of man by appearing to him directly, keeping him, as it were, close to his hand, and teaching him by direct and open revelation. That as time went on, God left men more and more to themselves outwardly: but only that he might raise their minds to higher notions of religion—that he might make them live by faith, and not merely by sight; and obey him of their own hearty free will, and not merely from fear or wonder. And therefore, in these days, when miraculous appearances have, as far as we know, entirely ceased, yet God is not changed. He is still as near as ever to men; still caring for them, still teaching them; and his very stopping of all miracles, so far from being a sign of God's anger or neglect, is a part of his gracious plan for the training of his Church.

For consider—Man was first put upon this earth, with all things round him new and strange to him; seeing himself weak and unarmed before the wild beasts of the forest, not even sheltered from the cold, as they are; and yet feeling in himself a power of mind, a cunning, a courage, which made him the lord of all the beasts by virtue of his *mind*, though they were stronger than he in body. All that we read of Adam and Eve in the Bible is, as we should expect, the history of *children*—children in mind, even when they were full-grown in stature. Innocent as children, but, like children, greedy, fanciful, ready to disobey at the first temptation, for the very silliest of reasons; and disobeying accordingly. Such creatures—with such wonderful powers lying hid in them, such a glorious future before them; and yet so weak, so wilful, so ignorant, so unable to take care of themselves, liable to be destroyed off the face of the earth by their own folly, or even by the wild beasts around—surely they needed some special and tender care from God to keep them from perishing at the very outset, till they had learned somewhat how to take care of themselves, what their business and duty were upon this earth. They needed it before they fell; they needed it still more, and their children likewise, after they fell: and if they needed it, we may trust God that he afforded it to them.

But again. Whence came this strange notion, which man alone has of all the living things which we see, of *Religion?* What put into the mind of man that strange imagination of beings greater than himself, whom he could not always see, but who might appear to him? What put into his mind the strange imagination that these unseen beings were more or less his *masters?* That they had made laws for him which he must obey? That he must honour and worship them, and do them service, in order that they might be favourable to him, and help, and bless, and teach him?

All nations except a very few savages (and we do not know but that their forefathers had it like the rest of mankind) have had some such notion as this; some idea of religion, and of a moral law of right and wrong.

Where did they get it?

Where, I ask again, did they get it?

My friends, after much thought I answer, there is no explanation of that question so simple, so rational, so probable, as the one which the text gives.

'And they heard the voice of the Lord God.'

Some, I know, say that man thought out for himself, in his own reason, the notion of God; that he by searching found out God. But surely that is contrary to all experience. Our experience is, that men left to themselves forget God; lose more and more all thought of God, and the unseen world; believe more and more in nothing but what they can see and taste and handle, and become as the beasts that perish. How then did man, who now is continually forgetting God, contrive to remember God for himself at first? How, unless God himself showed himself to man? I know some will say, that mankind invented for themselves false gods at first, and afterwards cleared and purified their own notions, till they discovered the true God. My friends, there is a homely old proverb which will well apply here. If there had been no gold guineas, there would be no brass ones. If men had not first had a notion of a true God, and then gradually lost it, they would not have invented false gods to supply his place. And whence did they get, I ask again, the notion of gods at all? The simplest answer is in the Bible: God taught them. I can find no better. I do not believe a better will ever be found.

And why not?

Why not? I ask. To say that God cannot appear to men is simply silly; for it is limiting God's Almighty power. He that made man and all heaven and earth, cannot he show himself to man, if he shall so please? To say that God will not appear to man because man is so insignificant, and this earth such a paltry little speck in the heavens, is to limit God's goodness; nay, it is to show that a man knows not what goodness means. What grace, what virtue is there higher than condescension? Then if God be, as he is, perfectly good, must he not be perfectly condescending—ready and willing to stoop to man, and all the more ready and the more willing, the more weak, igno-

rant, and sinful this man is? In fact, the greater
need man has of God, the more certain is it that
God will help him in that need.

Yes, my friends, the Bible is the revelation of
a God who condescends to men, and therefore
descends to men. And the more a man's reason
is spiritually enlightened to know the meaning
of goodness and holiness and justice and love,
the more simple, reasonable, and credible will it
seem to him that God at first taught men in the
days of their early ignorance, by the only method
by which (as far as we can conceive) he could have
taught them about himself; namely, by appearing
in visible shape, or speaking with audible voice;
and just as reasonable and credible, awful and
unfathomable mystery though it is, will be the
greater news, that that same Lord at last so con-
descended to man that he was conceived by the
Holy Ghost; born of the Virgin Mary; suffered
under Pontius Pilate; was crucified, dead, and
buried; and rose the third day, and ascended
into heaven. Credible and reasonable, not indeed
to the natural man who looks only at nature,
which he can see and hear and handle; but
credible and reasonable enough to the spiritual
man, whose mind has been enlightened by the

Spirit of God, to see that the things which are seen are temporal, but the things which are not seen are eternal ; even justice and love, mercy and condescension, the divine order, and the kingdom of the Living God.

And now one word on a matter which is tormenting the minds of many just now. It is often said that all that I have been saying is contrary to science. That this science and understanding of the world around us, which has improved so marvellously in our days, proves that the apparitions and miracles spoken of in the Bible cannot be true ; that God, or the angels of God, can never have walked with man in visible shape.

Now, my friends, I do not believe this. I believe the very contrary. I entreat you to set your minds at rest on this point; and to believe (what is certainly true) there is nothing in this new science to contradict the good old creed, that the Lord God of old appeared to his human children. It would take too much time, of course, to give you my reasons for saying this: and I must therefore ask you to take on trust from me when I tell you solemnly and earnestly that there is nothing in modern science which can, if rightly understood, contradict the glorious words of St. Paul, that God at sundry times and in divers manners spake to the fathers by the prophets, and hath at last spoken unto us by a Son, whom he hath appointed heir of all things: by whom also he made the worlds, who is the brightness of his glory, and the express image of his person, and upholdeth all things by the word of his power: even Jesus Christ, God blessed for ever. Amen.

What then shall we think of these things? Shall we say, ' How much better off were our forefathers than we! Ah, that we were not left to ourselves! Ah, that we lived in the good old times when God and his angels walked with men !'

My friends, what says Solomon the Wise?— ' Inquire not why the former times were better than these, for thou dost not inquire wisely concerning this.'

It is very natural for us to think that we could become more easily good men, more certain of going to heaven, if we saw divine apparitions and heard divine voices. A very natural thought. But *natural* things are not always the best or wisest things. Spiritual things are surely higher and deeper than natural things. It is natural to wish to see Christ, or some heavenly being, with our natural eyes and senses. But it is spiritual and therefore better for our souls, to be content to see him by faith, with the spiritual eyes of our heart and mind, to love him with all our heart and mind and soul, to worship him, to put our whole trust in him, to call upon him, to honour his holy name and his word, and to serve him truly all the days of our life.

Natural, indeed, to wish that we were back again in the old times. But we must recollect that these old times were not good times, but bad times, and for that very reason the Lord took pity on them. That they were times of darkness, and therefore it was that the people who sat in great darkness, and in the valley of the shadow of death, were allowed to see a great light. And that after that, the fulness of time, the very time which the Lord chose that he might be incarnate of the Virgin Mary, and came down upon this earth in human form, was not a good time. On the contrary, the fulness of time, 1863 years ago, was the very wickedest, most faithless, most unjust time that the world had ever seen—a time of which St. Paul said that there were none who did good, no, not one; that adders' poison was under all lips, and all feet swift to shed blood, and that the way of peace none had known.

Better, far better, to live in times like these, in which there is (among Christian nations at least) no great darkness, even though there be no great light; times in which the knowledge of the true God and his Son Jesus Christ is spreading, slowly but surely, over all the earth; and with it, the fruit of the knowledge of the Lord, justice, mercy, charity, fellow-feeling, and a desire to teach and improve all mankind, such as the world never saw before. These are the fruits of the Scriptures of the Lord, and the Sacraments of the Lord, and of the Holy Spirit of the Lord; and if that Holy Spirit be in our hearts, and we yield our hearts to his gracious motions and obey them, then we are really nearer to the Lord Jesus Christ than if we saw him, as Adam did, with our bodily eyes, and yet rebelled against him, as Adam did, in our hearts, and disobeyed him in our actions. Of old the Lord treated men as babes, and showed himself to their bodily eyes, that so they might learn that he was, and that he was near them. But us he treats as grown men, who know that he is, and that he is with us to the end of the world. And if he treats us as men, my friends, let us behave ourselves like men, and not like silly children, who cannot be trusted by themselves for a moment lest they do wrong or come to harm. Let us obey God, not with eye-service, just as long as we fancy that his eye is on us, but with the deeper, more spiritual, more honourable obedience of faith. Let us obey him for obedience' sake, and honour him for very honour's sake, as the young emigrant in foreign lands obeys and honours the parents whom he will never see again on earth; and let us look forward, like him, to the day when him whom we cannot see on earth we may, perhaps, be permitted to see in heaven, as the reward— and for what higher reward can man wish?—of faith and obedience.

SERMON IV.

NOAH'S FLOOD.

(Quinquagesima Sunday.)

GENESIS ix. 13.

I do set my bow in the cloud, and it shall be for a token of a covenant between me and the earth.

WE all know the history of Noah's flood. What have we learnt from that history? What were we intended to learn from it? What thoughts should we have about it?

There are many thoughts which we may have. We may think how the flood came to pass; what means God used to make it rain forty days; what is meant by breaking up the fountains of the great deep. We may calculate how large the ark was; and whether the Bible really means that it held all kinds of living things in the world, or only those of Noah's own country, or the animals which had been tamed and made useful to man. We may read long arguments as to whether the flood spread over the whole world, or only over the country where Noah and the rest of the sons of Adam then lived. We may puzzle ourselves concerning the rainbow of which the text speaks. How it was to be a sign of a covenant from God. Whether man had ever seen a rainbow before. Whether there had ever been rain before in Noah's country; or whether he did not live in that land of which the second chapter of Genesis says that the Lord had not caused it to rain upon the earth, but there went up a mist from the earth and watered the face of the ground, as it does still in that high land in the centre of Asia, in which old traditions put the garden of Eden, and from which, as far as we yet know, mankind came at the beginning.

We may puzzle our minds with these and a hundred more curious questions, as learned men have done in all ages. But—shall we become really the wiser by so doing? More learned we may become. But being learned and being wise are two different things. True wisdom is that which makes a man a better man. And will such puzzling questions and calculations as these, settle them how we may, ·make us *better* men ? Will they make us more honest and just, more generous and loving, more able to keep our tempers and control our appetites? I cannot see that. Will it make us better men merely to know that there was once a flood of waters on the earth? I cannot see that. If we look at the hills of sand and gravel round us, a little common sense will show us that there have been many floods of waters on the earth, long, long before the one of which the Bible speaks: but shall we be better men for knowing that either? I cannot see why we should. Now the Bible was sent to make us better men. How then will the history of the flood do that?

Easily enough, my friends, if we will listen to the Bible, and thinking less about the flood itself, think more about him who, so the Bible tells us, sent the flood.

The Bible, I have told you, is the revelation of the living Lord God, even Jesus Christ; who, in his turn, reveals to us the Father. And what we have to think of is, how does this story of the flood reveal, unveil to us the living Lord of the world, and his living government thereof? Let us look at the matter in that way, instead of puzzling ourselves with questions of words and endless genealogies which minister strife. Let us look at the matter in that way, instead of (like too many men now, and too many men in all ages) being so busy in picking to pieces the shell of the Bible, that we forget that the Bible has any kernel, and so let it slip through our hands. Let us look at the matter in that way, as a revelation of the living God, and then we shall find the history of the flood full of godly doctrine, and profitable for these times, and for all times whatsoever.

God sent a flood on the earth.

True; but the important matter is that *God* sent it.

God set the rainbow in the cloud, for a token.

True; but the important matter is that *God* set it there.

Important? Yes. What more important than to know that the flood did not come of itself, that the rainbow did not come of itself, and therefore that no flood comes of itself, no rainbow comes of itself; nothing comes of itself, but all comes straight and immediately from the one Living Lord God?

A man may say, But the flood must have been caused by clouds and rain; and there must have been some special natural cause for their falling at that place and that time?

What of that?

Or that the fountains of the great deep must have been broken up by natural earthquakes, such as break up the crust of the earth now.

What of that?

Or that the rainbow must have been caused by the sun's rays shining through rain-drops at a certain angle, as all rainbows are now. What of that? Very probably it was: but if not, What of that? What we ought to know, and what we ought to care for is, what the Bible tells us without a doubt, that however they came, God sent them. However they were made, God made them. Their manner, their place, their time was appointed exactly by God for a *moral* purpose. To do something for the immortal souls of men; to punish sinners; to preserve the righteous; to teach Noah and his children after him a moral lesson, concerning righteousness and sin; concerning the wrath of God against sin; concerning God, that he governs the world and all in it, and does not leave the world, or mankind, to go on of themselves and by themselves.

You see, I trust, what a message this was, and is, and ever will be for men; what a message and good news it must have been especially for the heathen of old time.

For what would the heathen, what actually did the heathen think about such sights as a flood, or a rainbow?

They thought of course that some one sent the flood. Common sense taught them that.

But what kind of person must he be, thought they, who sent the flood? Surely a very dark, terrible, angry God, who was easily and suddenly provoked to drown their cattle and flood their lands.

But the rainbow, so bright and gay, the sign of coming fine weather, could not belong to the same God who made the flood. What the fancies of the heathen about the rainbow were matters little to us: but they fancied, at least, that it belonged to some cheerful, bright and kind God. And so with other things. Whatever was bright, and beautiful, and wholesome in the world, like the rainbow, belonged to kind gods; whatever was dark, ugly, and destroying, like the flood, belonged to angry gods.

Therefore those of the heathen who were religious never felt themselves safe. They were always afraid of having offended some god, they knew not how; always afraid of some god turning against them, and bringing diseases against their bodies ; floods, drought, blight against their crops; storms against their ships, in revenge for some slight or neglect of theirs.

And all the while they had no clear notion that these gods made the world ; they thought that the gods were parts of the world, just as men are, and that beyond the gods there was the some sort of Fate, or necessity, which even gods must obey.

Do you not see now what a comfort—what a spring of hope, and courage, and peace of mind, and patient industry—it must have been to the men of old time to be told, by this story of the flood, that the God who sends the flood sends the rainbow also? There are not two gods, nor many gods, but one God, of whom are all things. Light and darkness, storm or sunshine, barrenness or wealth, come alike from him. Diseases, storm, flood, blight, all these show that there is in God an awfulness, a sternness, an anger if need be— a power of destroying his own work, of altering his own order ; but sunshine, fruitfulness, peace, and comfort, all show that love and mercy, beauty and order, are just as much attributes of his essence as awfulness and anger.

They tell us he is a God whose will is to love, to bless, to make his creatures happy, if they will allow him. They tell us that his anger is not a capricious, revengeful, proud, selfish anger, such as that of the heathen gods: but that it is an orderly anger, a just anger, a loving anger, and therefore an anger which in its wrath can remember mercy. Out of God's wrath shineth love, as the rainbow out of the storm; if it repenteth him that he hath made man, it is only because man is spoiling and ruining himself, and wasting the gifts of the good world by his wickedness. If he see fit to destroy man out of the earth, he will destroy none but those who deserve and need destroying. He will save those whom, like Noah, he can trust to begin afresh, and raise up a better race of men to do his work in the world. If God send a flood to destroy all living things, any when or anywhere, he will show, by putting the rainbow in the cloud, that floods and destruction and anger are not his rule; that his rule is sunshine, and peace, and order; that though he found it necessary once to curse the ground, once to sweep away a wicked race of men, yet that even that was, if one dare use the words of God, against his gracious will; that his will was from the beginning, peace on earth, and not floods, and good will to men, and not destruction; and that in his *heart*, in the abyss of his essence, and of which it is written, that God is Love—in his heart I say, he said, 'I will not again curse the ground any more for man's sake, even though the imagination of man's heart is evil from his youth. Neither will I again smite everything living, as I have done. While the earth remaineth, seed-time and harvest, summer and winter, and day and night, shall not cease.'

This is the God which the book of Genesis goes on revealing and unveiling to us more and more—a God in whom men may *trust*.

The heathen could not trust their gods. The Bible tells men of a God whom they can trust. That is just the difference between the Bible and all other books in the world. But what a difference! Difference enough to make us say, Sooner that every other book in the world were lost, and the Bible preserved, than that we should lose the Bible, and with the Bible lose faith in God.

And now, my friends, what shall we learn from this?

What shall we learn? Have we not learnt enough already? If we have learnt something more of who God is; if we have learnt that he is a God in whom we can trust through joy and sorrow, through light and darkness, through life and death, have we not learnt enough for ourselves? Yes, if even those poor and weak words about God which I have just spoken, could go home into all your hearts, and take root, and bear fruit there, they would give you a peace of mind, a comfort, a courage among all the chances and changes of this mortal life, and a hope for the life to come, such as no other news which man can tell you will ever give. But there is one special lesson which we may learn from the history of the flood, of which I may as well tell you at once. The Bible account of the flood will teach us how to look at the many terrible accidents, as we foolishly call them, which happen still upon this earth. There are floods still, here and there, earthquakes, fires, fearful disasters, like that great colliery disaster of last year, which bring death, misery and ruin to thousands. The Bible tells us what to think of them, when it tells us of the flood.

Do I mean that these disasters come as punishments to the people who are killed by them? That is exactly what I do *not* mean. It was true of the flood. It is true, no doubt, in many other cases. But our blessed Lord has specially forbidden *us* to settle when it is true to say that any particular set of people are destroyed for their sins: forbidden *us* to say that the poor creatures who perish in this way are worse than their neighbours.

'Thinkest thou,' he says, 'that those Galilæans whose blood Pilate mingled with their sacrifices, were sinners above all the Galilæans? Or those eighteen, on whom the tower in Siloam fell, and killed them; think you that they were sinners above all who dwelt in Jerusalem? I tell you nay.'

'Judge not,' he says, 'and ye shall not be judged,' and therefore we must not judge. We have no right to say, for instance, that the terrible earthquake in Italy, two years ago, came as a punishment for the sins of the people. We have no right to say that the twenty or thirty thousand human beings, with innocent children among them by hundreds, who were crushed or swallowed up by that earthquake in a few hours, were sinners above all that dwelt in Italy. We must not say that, for the Lord God himself has forbidden it.

But this we may say (for God himself has said it in the Bible), that these earthquakes, and all other disasters, great or small, do not come of themselves—do not come by accident, or chance, or blind necessity; but that he *sends* them, and that they fulfil his will and word.   He sends them, and therefore they do not come in vain.   They fulfil his will, and his will is a good will.   They carry out his purpose, but his purpose is a gracious purpose.   God may send them in anger; but in his anger he remembers mercy, and his very wrath to some is part and parcel of his love to the rest. Therefore these disasters must be meant to do good, and will do good to mankind.   They may be meant to teach men, to warn them, to make them more wise and prudent for the future, more humble and aware of their own ignorance and weakness, more mindful of the frailty of human life, that remembering that in the midst of life we are in death, they may seek the Lord while he may be found, and call upon him while he is near.   They may be meant to do that, and to do a thousand things more.   For God's ways are not as our ways, or his thoughts as our thoughts. His ways are unsearchable, and his paths past finding out.   Who hath known the mind of the Lord, that he may instruct him, or even settle what the Lord means by doing this or that?

All we can say is—and that is a truly blessed

thing to be able to say—that floods and earthquakes, fire and storms, come from the Lord
whose name is Love; the same Lord who walked
with Adam in the garden, who brought the children
of Israel out of Egypt, who was born on earth
of the Virgin Mary, who shed his life-blood for
sinful man, who wept over Jerusalem even when
he was about to destroy it so that not one stone
was left on another, and who, when he looked
on the poor little children of Judæa, untaught
or mistaught, enslaved by the Romans, and but
too likely to perish or be carried away captive
in the fearful war which was coming on their
land, said of them, 'It is not the will of your
Father in heaven, that one of these little ones
shall perish.'　Him at least we can trust, in the
dark and dreadful things of this world, as well
as in the bright and cheerful ones; and say
with Job, 'Though he slay me, yet will I trust
in him. I have received good from the hands
of the Lord, and shall I not receive evil?'

SERMON V.

ABRAHAM.

(First Sunday in Lent.)

GENESIS xvii. 1, 2.

And when Abram was ninety years old and nine, the Lord appeared
to Abram, and said unto him, I am the Almighty God; walk
before me, and be thou perfect.

I HAVE told you that the Bible reveals, that is,
unveils the Lord God, Jesus Christ our Lord,
and through him God the Father Almighty. I
have tried to show you how the Bible does so, step
by step. I go on to show you another step which
the Bible takes, and which explains much that has
gone before.

From whom did Moses and the holy men of old
whom Moses taught get their knowledge of God,
the true God?

The answer seems to be—from Abraham.

God taught Moses more, much more than he

taught Abraham. It was Moses who bade men
call God Jehovah, the I AM; but who, hundreds
of years before, taught them to call him the Almighty God?

The answer seems to be, Abraham. God, we
read, appeared to Abraham, and said to him, 'Get
thee out of thy country, and from thy father's
house, unto a land that I shall show thee, and I
will make of thee a great nation.' And again the
Lord said to him, 'I am the Almighty God, walk
before me and be thou perfect, and thou shalt be a
father of many nations.'

'And Abraham believed God, and it was counted
to him for righteousness. And he was called the
friend of God.'

But from what did Abraham turn to worship the
living God? From idols? We are not certain.
There is little or no mention of idols in Abraham's
time. He worshipped, more probably, the host of
heaven, the sun and moon and stars. So say the
old traditions of the Arabs, who are descended
from Abraham through Ishmael, and so it is most
likely to have been. That was the temptation in
the East. You read again and again how his
children, the Jews, turned back from God to worship the host of heaven; and that false worship

seems to have crept in at some very early time. The sun, you must remember, and the moon are far more brilliant and powerful in the East than here; their power of doing harm or good to human beings and to the crops of the land is far greater; while the stars shine in the East with a brightness of which we here have no notion. We do not know, in this cloudy climate, what St. Paul calls the glory of the stars; nor see how much one star differs from another star in glory; and therefore here in the North we have never been tempted to worship them as the Easterns were. The sun, the moon, the stars, were the old gods of the East, the Elohim, the high and mighty ones, who ruled over men, over their good and bad fortunes, over the weather, the cattle, the crops, sending burning drought, pestilence, sun-strokes, and those moon-strokes which we never have here; but of which the Psalmist speaks when he says, 'The sun shall not smite thee by day, neither the moon by night.' And them the old Easterns worshipped in some wild confused way.

But to Abraham it was revealed that the sun, the moon, and the stars were not Elohim—the high and mighty Ones. That there was but one Elohim, one high and mighty One, the Almighty maker of

them all. He did not learn that, perhaps, at once.
Indeed the Bible tells us how God taught him step
by step, as he teaches all men, and revealed
himself to him again and again, till he had taught
Abraham all that he was to know. But he did
teach him this; as a beautiful old story of the
Arabs sets forth. They say how (whether before
or after God called him, we cannot tell) Abraham
at night saw a star: and he said, 'This is my Lord.'
But when the star set, he said, 'I like not those
who vanish away.' And when he saw the moon
rising, he said, 'This is my Lord.' But when the
moon too set, he said, 'Verily, if my Lord direct
me not in the right way, I shall be as one who
goeth astray.' But when he saw the sun rising, he
said, 'This is my Lord: this is greater than star or
moon.' But the sun went down likewise. Then
said Abraham, 'O my people, I am clear of these
things. I turn my face to him who hath made the
heaven and the earth.'

And was this all that Abraham believed—that
the sun and moon and stars were not gods, but
that there was a God besides, who had made them
all? My friends, there have been thousands and
tens of thousands since, I fear, who have believed
as much as that, and yet who cannot call Abraham

their spiritual father, who are not justified by faith with faithful Abraham.

For merely to believe that, is a dead faith, which will never be counted for righteousness, because it will never make man a righteous man doing righteous and good deeds as Abraham did.

Of Abraham it is written, that what he knew, he did. That his faith wrought with his works. And by his works his faith was made perfect. That when he gained faith in God, he went and acted on his faith. When God called him he went out, not knowing whither he went.

His faith is only shown by his works. Because he believed in God he went and did things which he would not have done if he had not believed in God. Of him it is written, that he obeyed the voice of the Lord, and kept his charge, his commandments, his statutes, and his laws.

In a word, he had not merely found out that there was one God, but that that one God was a good God, a God whom he must obey, and obey by being a good man. Therefore his faith was counted to him for righteousness, because it *was* righteousness, and made him do righteous deeds.

He believed that God was helping him ; therefore he had no need to oppress or overreach any man. He believed that God's eye was on him; therefore he dared not oppress or overreach any man.

His faith in God made him brave. He went forth he knew not whither; but he had put his trust in God, and he did not fear. He and his three hundred slaves, born in his house, were not afraid to set out against the four Arab kings who had just conquered the five kings of the vale of Jordan, and plundered the whole land. Abraham and his little party of faithful slaves follow them for miles, and fall on them and defeat them utterly, setting the captives free, and bringing back all the plunder; and then, in return for all that he has done, Abraham will take nothing—not even, he says, 'a thread or a shoe-latchet—lest men should say, We have made Abraham rich.' And why?

Because his faith in God made him high-minded, generous, and courteous; as when he bids Lot go whither he will with his flocks and herds. 'Let there be no strife, I pray thee, between thee and me. If thou wilt take the left hand, I will go to the right.' He is then, as again with the king of Sodom, and with the three strangers at the tent door, and with the children of Heth, when he is buying the cave of Machpelah for a burying-place for Sarah—always and everywhere the same courteous, self-restrained, high-bred, high-minded man.

It has been said that true religion will make a man a more thorough gentleman than all the courts in Europe. And it is true: you may see simple labouring men as thorough gentlemen as any duke, simply because they have learned to fear God; and fearing him, to restrain themselves, and to think of other people more than of themselves, which is the very root and essence of all good breeding. And such a man was Abraham of old —a plain man, dwelling in tents, helping to tend his own cattle, fetching in the calf from the field himself, and dressing it for his guests with his own hand; but still, as the children of Heth said of him, a mighty prince—not merely in wealth of flocks and herds, but a prince in manners and a prince in heart.

But faith in God did more for Abraham than this: it made him a truly pious man—it made him the friend of God.

There were others in Abraham's days who had some knowledge of the one true God. Lot his nephew, Abimelech, Aner, Eshcol, Mamre, and others, seem to have known whom Abraham meant when he spoke of the Almighty God. But of Abraham alone it is said that he believed God; that he trusted in God, and rested on him; was built up on God; rested on God as a child in the mother's arms—for this we are told, is the full meaning of the word in the Bible—and looked to God as his shield and his exceeding great reward. He trusted in God utterly, and it was counted to him for righteousness.

And of Abraham alone it is said that he was the friend of God; that God spoke with him, and he with God. He first of all men of whom we read, at least since the time of Adam, knew what communion with God meant; knew that God spoke to him as a friend, a benefactor, a preserver, who was teaching and training him with a father's love and care; and felt that he in return could answer God, could open his heart to him, tell him not only of his wants, but of his doubts and fears.

Yes, we may almost say, on the strength of the Bible, that Abraham was the first human being, as far as we know, who prayed with his heart and soul; who knew what true prayer means—the prayer of the heart, by which man draws near to God, and finds that God is near to him. This —this communion with God, is the especial glory of Abraham's character. This it is which has given him his name through all generations, The friend of God. Or, as his descendants the Arabs call him to this day, simply, 'The Friend.'

This it is which gained him the name of the Father of the Faithful; the father of all who believe, whether they be descended from him, or whether they be, like us, of a different nation. This it is which has made a wise man say of Abraham, that if we will consider what he knew and did, and in what a dark age he lived, we shall see that Abraham may be (unless we except Moses) the greatest of mere human beings—that the human race may owe more to him than to any mortal man.

But why need we learn from Abraham? we who, being Christians, know and believe the true faith so much more clearly than Abraham could do.

Ah, my friends, it is easier to know than to believe, and easier to know than to do. Easier to talk of Abraham's faith than to have Abraham's faith. Easier to preach learned and orthodox sermons about how Abraham was justified by his faith, than to be justified ourselves by our own faith.

And say not in your hearts, 'It was easy for

Abraham to believe God. I should have believed
of course in his place. If God spoke to me, of
course I should obey him.' My friends, there is
no greater and no easier mistake. God has spoken
to many a man who has not believed him, neither
obeyed him, and so he may to you. God spoke
to Abraham, and he believed him and obeyed him.
And why? Because there was in Abraham's heart
something which there is not in all men's hearts—
something which *answered* to God's call, and made
him certain that the call was from God—even the
Holy Spirit of God.

So God may call you, and you may obey him,
if only the Spirit of God be in you ; but not else.
May call you, did I say? God *does* call you and
me, does speak to us, does command us, far more
clearly than he did Abraham. We know the
mystery of Christ, which in other ages was *not*
made known to the sons of men as it is now revealed to his holy apostles and prophets by the
Spirit. God, who at sundry times and in divers
manners spoke to the fathers by the prophets, hath
in these last days spoken to us by his *Son*, Jesus
Christ our Lord, and told us our duty, and the
reward which doing our duty will surely bring, far
more clearly than ever he did to Abraham.

But do we listen to him? Do we say with Abraham, 'O my people, I am clear of all these things which rise and set, which are born and die, which begin and end in time, and turn my face to him that made heaven and earth!' If so, how is it that we see people everywhere worshipping not idols of wood and stone, but other things, all manner of things beside God, and saying, 'These are my Elohim. These are the high and mighty ones whom I must obey. These are the strong things on which depend my fortune and my happiness. I must obey *them* first, and let plain doing right and avoiding wrong come after as it can.'

One worships the laws of trade, and says, 'I know this and that is hardly right; but it is in the way of business, and therefore I must do it.'

One worships public opinion, and follows after the multitude to do evil, doing what he knows is wrong, simply because others do it, and it is the way of the world.

One worships the interest of his party, whether in religion or in politics; and does for their sake mean and false, cruel and unjust things, which he would not do for his own private interest.

Too many, even in a free country, worship great people, and put their trust in princes, saying, 'I am sorry to have to do this. I know it is rather mean ; but I must, or I shall lose such and such a great man's interest and favour.' Or, 'I know I cannot afford this expense ; but if I do not I shall not get into good society, and this person and that will not ask me to his house.'

All, meanwhile, except a few, rich or poor, worship money ; and believe more or less, in spite of the Lord's solemn warning to the contrary, that a man's life does consist in the abundance of the things which he possesses.

These are the Elohim of this world, the high and mighty things to which men turn for help instead of to the living God, who was before all things, and will be after them ; and behold they vanish away, and where then are those that have put their trust in them ?

But blessed is he whose trust is in God the Almighty, and whose hope is in the Lord Jehovah, the eternal I Am. Blessed is he who, like faithful Abraham, says to his family, 'My people, I am clear of all these things. I turn my face from them to him who hath made earth and heaven. I go through this world like Abraham, not knowing whither I go ; but like Abraham, I fear not, for I go whither God sends me. I rest on God ; he is

my defence, and my exceeding great reward. To
have known him, loved him, obeyed him, is reward
enough, even if I do not, as the world would say,
succeed in life. Therefore I long not for power
and honour, riches and pleasure. I am content
to do my duty faithfully in that station of life
to which God has called me, and to be forgiven for
all my failings and shortcomings for the sake of
Jesus Christ our Lord, and that is enough for me ;
for I believe in my Father in heaven, and believe
that he knows best for me and for my children.
He has not promised me, as he promised Abraham,
to make of me a great nation; but he has promised
that the righteous man shall never be deserted, or
his children beg their bread. He has promised to
keep his covenant and mercy to a thousand generations with those who keep his commandments and
do them ; and that is enough for me. In God
have I put my trust, and I will not fear what man,
or earth, or heaven, or any created thing can do
unto me.'

Blessed is that man, whether he inherit honourably great estates from his ancestors, or whether
he make honourably great wealth and station for
himself; whether he spend his life quietly and
honestly in the country farm or in the village shop,

or whether he simply earn his bread from week to week by plough and spade. Blessed is he, and blessed are his children after him. For he is a son of Abraham; and of him God hath said, as of Abraham, ' I know him that he will command his children and household after him, and they shall keep the way of the Lord, to do justice and judgment, that the Lord may bring on him the blessing which he has spoken.'

Yes; blessed is that man. He has chosen his share of Abraham's faith; and he and his children after him shall have their share of Abraham's blessing.

SERMON VI.

JACOB AND ESAU.

(Second Sunday in Lent.)

GENESIS XXV. 29—34.

> And Jacob sod pottage : and Esau came from the field, and he was
> faint : And Esau said to Jacob, Feed me, I pray thee, with
> that same red pottage ; for I am faint : therefore was his name
> called Edom. And Jacob said, Sell me this day thy birthright.
> And Esau said, Behold, I am at the point to die : and what
> profit shall this birthright do to me? And Jacob said, Swear
> to me this day ; and he sware unto him : and he sold his birth-
> right unto Jacob. Then Jacob gave Esau bread and pottage of
> lentiles ; and he did eat and drink, and rose up, and went his
> way : thus Esau despised his birthright.

I HAVE been telling you of late that the Bible is the revelation of God. But how does the story of Jacob and Esau reveal God to us? What further lesson concerning God do we learn there-from?

I think that if we will take the story simply as it stands we shall see easily enough. For it is all simple and natural enough. Jacob and Esau, we shall see, were men of like passions with ourselves ; men as we are, mixed up of good and evil, sometimes right and sometimes wrong : and God rewarded them when they did right, and punished them when they did wrong, just as he does with us now.

They were men, though, of very different characters : we may see men like them now every day round us. Esau, we read, was a hunter—a man of the field ; a bold, fierce, active man ; generous, brave, and kind-hearted, as the end of his story shows : but with just the faults which such a man would have. He was hasty, reckless, and fond of pleasure ; passionate too, and violent. Have we not seen just such men again and again, and liked them for what was good in them, and been sorry too that they were not more sober and reasonable, and true to themselves ?

Jacob was the very opposite kind of man. He was a plain man—what we call a still, solid, prudent, quiet man—and a dweller in tents : he lived peaceably, looking after his father's flocks and herds ; while Esau liked better the sport and danger of hunting wild beasts, and bringing home venison to his father.

Now Jacob, we see, was of course a more thoughtful man than Esau. He kept more quiet, and so had more time to think : and he had plainly thought a great deal over God's promise to his grandfather Abraham. He believed that God had promised Abraham that he would make his seed as the sand of the sea for multitude, and give them that fair land of Canaan, and that in his seed all the families of the earth should be ,blessed ; and that seemed to him, and rightly, a very grand and noble thing. And he set his heart on getting that blessing for himself, and supplanting his elder brother Esau, and being the heir of the promises in his stead. Well, —that was mean and base and selfish perhaps : but there is somewhat of an excuse for Jacob's conduct, in the fact that he and Esau were twins; that in one sense neither of them was older than the other. And you must recollect, that it was not at all a regular custom in the East for the eldest son to be his father's heir, as it is in England. You find that few or none of the great kings of the Jews were eldest sons. The custom was not kept up as it is here. So Jacob may have said to himself, and not have been very wrong in saying it:

'I have as good a right to the birthright as Esau. My father loves him best because he brings him in venison ; but I know the value of the honour which is before my family. Surely the one of us who cares most about the birthright will be most fit to have it, and ought to have it; and Esau cares nothing for it, while I do.'

So Jacob, in his cunning, bargaining way, took advantage of his brother's weak, hasty temper, and bought his birthright of him, as the text tells.

That story shows us what sort of a man Esau was: hasty, careless, fond of the good things of this life. He had no reason to complain if he lost his birthright. He did not care for it, and so he had thrown it away. Perhaps he forgot what he had done; but his sin found him out, as our sins are sure to find each of us out. The day came when he wanted his birthright and could not have it, and found no place for repentance—that is, no chance of undoing what he had done—though he sought it carefully with tears. He had sown, and he must reap; he had made his bed, and he must lie on it. And so must Jacob in his turn.

Now this, I think, is just what the story teaches us concerning God. God chooses Abraham's family to grow into a great nation, and to be a peculiar people. The next question will be: If God favours that family, will he do unjust things to help them? —will he let them do unjust things to help themselves? The Bible answers positively, No. God will not be unjust or arbitrary in choosing one man and rejecting another. If he chooses Jacob, it is because Jacob is fit for the work which God wants done. If he rejects Esau, it is because Esau is not fit.

It is natural, I know, to pity poor Esau; but one has no right to do more. One has no right to fancy for a moment that God was arbitrary or hard upon him. Esau is not the sort of man to be the father of a great nation, or of anything else great. Greedy, passionate, reckless people like him, without due feeling of religion or of the unseen world, are not the men to govern the world, or help it forward, or be of use to mankind, or train up their families in justice and wisdom and piety. If there had been no people in the world but people like Esau, we should be savages at this day, without religion or civilization of any kind. They are of the earth, earthy; dust they are, and unto dust they will return. It is men like Jacob whom God chooses—men who have a feeling of religion and the unseen world; men who can look forward, and live by faith, and form plans for the future—and carry them out too, against disappointment and difficulty, till they succeed.

Look at one side of Jacob's character—his perseverance. He serves seven years for Rachel, because he loves her. Then when he is cheated, and Leah given him instead, he serves seven years more for Rachel—'and they seemed to him a short time, for the love he bore to her;' and then he serves seven years more for the flocks and herds. A slave, or little better than a slave, of his own free will, for one-and-twenty years, to get what he wanted. Those are the men whom God uses, and whom God prospers. Men with deep hearts and strong wills, who set their minds on something which they cannot see, and work steadfastly for it, till they get it; for God gives it to them in good time—when patience has had her perfect work upon their characters, and made them fit for success.

Esau, we find, got some blessing—the sort of blessing he was fit for. He loved his father, and he was rewarded. 'And Isaac his father answered and said unto him, Behold, thy dwelling shall be the fatness of the earth, and of the dew of heaven from above; and by thy sword shalt thou live, and shalt serve thy brother; and it shall come to pass when thou shalt have the dominion, that thou shalt break his yoke from off thy neck.'

He was a brave, generous-hearted man, in spite of his faults. He was to live the free hunter's life which he loved; and we find that he soon became the head of a wild powerful tribe, and his sons after him. Dukes of Edom they were called for several generations; but they never rose to any solid and lasting power; they never became a great nation, as Jacob's children did. They were just what one would expect—wild, unruly, violent people. They have long since perished utterly off the face of the earth.

And what did Jacob get, who so meanly bought the birthright, and cheated his father out of the blessing? Trouble in the flesh; vanity and vexation of spirit. He had to flee from his father's house; never to see his mother again; to wander over the deserts to kinsmen who cheated him as he had cheated others; to serve Laban for twenty-one years; to crouch miserably in fear and trembling, as a petitioner for his life before Esau whom he had wronged, and to be made more ashamed than ever, by finding that generous Esau had forgiven and forgotten all. Then to see his daughter brought to shame, his sons murderers, plotting against their own brother, his favourite son; to see his grey hairs going down with sorrow to the grave; to confess to Pharaoh, after one hundred and twenty years of life, that few and evil had been the days of his pilgrimage.

Then did his faith in God win no reward? Not so. That was his reward, to be chastened and punished, till his meanness was purged out of him. He had taken God for his guide; and God did guide him accordingly; though along a very different path from what he expected. God accepted his faith, delivered his soul, gave him rest and peace at last in his old age in Egypt, let him find his son Joseph again in power and honour: but all along God punished his own inventions—as he will punish yours and mine, my friends, all the while that he may be accepting our faith and delivering our souls, because we trust in him. So God rewarded Jacob by giving him more light: by not leaving him to himself, and his own darkness and meanness, but opening his eyes to understand the wondrous things of God's law, and showing him how God's law is everlasting, righteous, not to be escaped by any man; how every action brings forth its appointed fruit; how those who sow the wind will reap the whirlwind. Jacob's first notion was like the notion of the heathen in all times, ' My God has a special

favour for me, therefore I may do what I like. He
will prosper me in doing wrong; he will help me
to cheat my father.' But God showed him that
that was just not what he would do for him. He
would help and protect him; but only while he
was doing RIGHT. God would not alter his
moral laws for him or any man. God would be
just and righteous; and Jacob must be so likewise,
till he learnt to trust not merely in a God who
happened to have a special favour to him, but in
the righteous God who loves justice, and wishes
to make men righteous even as he is righteous,
and will make them righteous, if they trust in
him.

That was the reward of Jacob's faith—the best
reward which any man can have. He was taught
to know God, whom truly to know is everlasting
life. And this, it seems to me, is the great revelation concerning God which we learn from the
history of Jacob and Esau. That God, how much
soever favour he may show to certain persons, is
still, essentially and always, a *just* God.

And now, my friends, if any of you are tempted
to follow Jacob's example, take warning betimes.
You will be tempted. There are men among you
—there are in every congregation—who are, like

Jacob, sober, industrious, careful, prudent men, and fairly religious too; men who have the good sense to see that Solomon's proverbs are true, and that the way to wealth and prosperity is to fear God, and keep his commandments.

May you prosper; may God's blessing be upon your labour; may you succeed in life, and see your children well settled and thriving round you, and go down to the grave in peace.

But never forget, my good friends, that you will be tempted as Jacob was—to be dishonest. I cannot tell why; but professedly religious men, in all countries, in all religions, are, and always have been, tempted in that way—to be mean and cunning and false at times. It is so, and there is no denying it: when all other sins are shut out from them by their religious profession, and their care for their own character, and their fear of hell, the sin of lying, for some strange reason, is left open to them; and to it they are tempted to give way. For God's sake—for the sake of Christ, who was full of grace and truth—for your own sakes—struggle against that. Unless you wish to say at last with poor old Jacob, 'Few and evil have been the days of my pilgrimage;' struggle against that. If you fear God and believe that he is with you, God will prosper your plans and labour; but never make that an excuse for saying in your hearts, like Jacob, 'God intends that I should have these good things; therefore I may take them for myself by unfair means.' The birthright is yours. It is you, the steady, prudent, God-fearing ones, who will prosper on the earth, and not poor wild, hot-headed Esau. But do not make that an excuse for robbing and cheating Esau, because he is not as thoughtful as you are. The Lord made him as well as you; and died for him as well as for you; and wills his salvation as well as yours; and if you cheat him the Lord will avenge him speedily. If you give way to meanness, covetousness, falsehood, as Jacob did, you will rue it; the Lord will enter into judgment with you quickly, and all the more quickly because he loves you. Because there is some right in you—because you are on the whole on the right road—the Lord will visit you with disappointment and affliction, and make your own sins your punishment.

If you deceive other people, other people shall deceive you, as they did Jacob. If you lay traps, you shall fall into them yourselves, as Jacob did. If you fancy that because you trust in God,

God will overlook any sin in you, as Jacob did, you shall see, as Jacob did, that your sin shall surely find you out.   The Lord will be more sharp and severe with you than with Esau.   And why? Because he has given you more, and requires more of you; and therefore he will chastise you, and sift you like wheat, till he has parted the wheat from the tares.   The wheat is your faith, your belief that if you trust in God he will prosper you, body and soul.   That is God's good seed, which he has sown in you.   The tares are your fancies that you may do wrong and mean things to help yourselves, because God has an especial favour for you.   That is the devil's sowing, which God will burn out of you by the fire of affliction, as he did out of Jacob, and keep your faith safe, as good seed in his garner, for the use of your children after you, that you may teach them to walk in God's commandments and serve him in spirit and in truth.   For God is a God of truth, and no liar shall stand in his sight, let him be never so religious; he requires truth in the inward parts, and truth he will have; and whom he loves he will chasten, as he chastened Jacob of old, till he has made him understand that honesty is the best policy; and that whatever false prophets may tell you, there is not one law for the believer and another for the unbeliever; but whatsoever a man sows, that shall he reap, and receive the due reward of the deeds done in the body, whether they be good or evil.

SERMON VII.

JOSEPH.

(Preached on the Sunday before the Wedding of the Prince of Wales. March 8th, third Sunday in Lent.)

GENESIS xxxix. 9.

How can I do this great wickedness, and sin against God?

THE story of Joseph is one which will go home to all healthy hearts. Every child can understand, every child can feel with it. It is a story for all men and all times. Even if it had not been true, and not real fact, but a romance of man's invention, it would have been loved and admired by men; far more then, when we know that it is true, that it actually did so happen; that is part and parcel of the Holy Scriptures.

We all, surely, know the story—How Joseph's brethren envy him and sell him for a slave into Egypt—how there for a while he prospers—how his master's wife tempts him—how he is thrown into prison on her slander—how there again he prospers—how he explains the dreams of Pharaoh's servants—how he lies long forgotten in the prison—how at last Pharaoh sends for him to interpret a dream for him, and how he rises to power and great glory—how his brothers come down to Egypt to buy corn, and how they find him lord of all the land—how subtilly he tries them to see if they have repented of their old sin—how his heart yearns over them in spite of all their wickedness to him—how at last he reveals himself, and forgives them utterly, and sends for his poor old father Jacob down into Egypt. Whosoever does not delight in that story, simply as a story, whenever he hears it read, cannot have a wholesome human heart in him.

But why was this story of Joseph put into Holy Scripture, and at such length, too? It seems, at first sight, to be simply a family history—the story of brothers and their father; it seems, at first sight, to teach us nothing concerning our redemption and salvation; it seems, at first sight, not to reveal anything fresh to us concerning God; it seems, at first sight, not to be needed for the general plan of the Bible history. It tells us, of course, how the Israelites first came into Egypt; and that was necessary for us to know.

But the Bible might have told us that in ten verses. Why has it spent upon the story of Joseph and his brethren, not ten verses, but ten chapters?

Now we have a right to ask such questions as these, if we do not ask them out of any carping, fault-finding spirit, trying to pick holes in the Bible, from which God defend us and all Christian men. If we ask such questions in faith and reverence—that is, believing and taking for granted that the Bible is right, and respecting it, as the Book of books, in which our own forefathers and all Christian nations upon earth for many ages have found all things necessary for their salvation—if, I say, we question over the Bible in that child-like, simple, respectful spirit, which is the true spirit of wisdom and understanding, by which our eyes will be truly opened to see the wondrous things of God's law: then we may not only seek as our Lord bade us, but we shall find, as our Lord prophesied that we should. We shall find some good reason for this story of Joseph being so long, and find that the story of Joseph, like all the rest of the Bible, reveals a new lesson to us concerning God and the character of God.

I said that the story of Joseph looks, at first sight, to be merely a family history. But suppose that that were the very reason why it is in the Bible, because it is a family history. Suppose that families were very sacred things in the eyes of God. That the ties of husband and wife, parent and child, brother and sister, were appointed, not by man, but by God. Then would not Joseph's story be worthy of being in the Bible? Would it not, as I said it would, reveal something fresh to us concerning God and the character of God?

Consider now, my friends: Is it not one great difference—one of the very greatest—between men and beasts, that men live in families, and beasts do not? That men have the sacred family feeling, and beasts have not? They have the beginnings of it, no doubt. The mother, among beasts, feels love to her children, but only for a while. God has implanted in her something of that deepest, holiest, purest of all feelings—a mother's love. But as soon as her young ones are able to take care of themselves, they are nothing to her— among the lower animals, less than nothing. The fish or the crocodile will take care of her eggs jealously, and as soon as they are hatched, turn round and devour her own young.

The feeling of a *father* to his child, again, you find is fainter still among beasts. The father, as you all know, not only cares little for his offspring, even if he sometimes helps to feed them at first, but is often jealous of them, hates them, will try to kill them when they grow up.

Husband and wife, again : there is no sacredness between them among dumb animals. A lasting and an unselfish attachment, not merely in youth, but through old age and beyond the grave—what is there like this among the animals, except in the case of certain birds, like the dove and the eagle, who keep the same mate year after year, and have been always looked on with a sort of affection and respect by men for that very reason ?

But where, among beasts, do you ever find any trace of those two sacred human feelings—the love of brother to brother, or of child to father ? Where do you find the notion that the tie between husband and wife is a sacred thing, to be broken at no temptation, but in man ?

These are *the* feelings which man has alone of all living animals.

These then, remember, are the very family feelings which come out in the story of Joseph. He honours holy wedlock when he tells his master's wife, 'How can I do this great wickedness, and sin against God?' He honours his father, when he is not ashamed of him, wild shepherd out of the desert though he might be, and an abomination to the Egyptians, while he himself is now in power and wealth and glory, as a prince in a civilized country. He honours the tie of brother to brother, by forgiving and weeping over the very brothers who have sold him into slavery.

But what has all this to do with God?

Now man, as we know, is an animal with an immortal spirit in him. He has, as St. Paul so carefully explains to us, a flesh and a spirit—a flesh like the beasts which perish; a spirit which comes from God.

Now the Bible teaches us that man did not get these family feelings from his flesh, from the animal, brute part of him. They are not carnal, but spiritual. He gets them from his spirit, and they are inspired into him by the Spirit of God. They come not from the earth below, but from the heaven above; from the image of God, in which man alone of all living things was made.

For if it were not so, we should surely see some family feeling in the beasts which are most like men. But we do not. In the apes, which are, in their shape and fleshly nature, so strangely and shockingly like human beings, there is not as much family feeling as there is in many birds, or even insects. Nay, the wild negroes, among whom they live, hold them in abhorrence, and believe that they were once men like themselves, who were gradually changed into brute beasts, by giving way to detestable sins; while these very negroes themselves, heathens and savages as they are, *have* the family feeling—the feeling of husband for wife, father for child, brother for brother; not, indeed, as strongly and purely as we, or at least those of us who are really Christian and civilized, but still they have it; and that makes between the lowest man and the highest brute a difference which I hold is as wide as the space between heaven and earth.

It is man alone, I say, who has the idea of family; and who has, too, the strange, but most true belief that these family ties are appointed by God—that they are a part of his religion—that in breaking them, by being an unfaithful husband, a dishonest servant, an unnatural son, a selfish brother, he sins, not only against man, and man's order and laws, but against God.

Parent and child, brother and sister—those ties

are not of the earth earthy, but of the heaven of God, eternal. They may begin in time; of what happened before we came into this world we know nought. But having begun, they cannot end. Of what will happen after we leave this world, that at least we know in part.

Parent and child; brother and sister; husband and wife likewise; these are no ties of man's invention. They are ties of God's binding; they are patterns and likenesses of his substance, and of his being. Of the eternal Father, who says for ever to the eternal Son, 'This day have I begotten *thee.*' Of the Son who says for ever to the Father, 'I come to do thy will, O God.' Of the Son of God, Jesus Christ, who is not ashamed to call us his brethren; but like a greater Joseph, was sent before by God to save our lives with a great deliverance when our forefathers were but savages and heathens. Husband and wife likewise—are not they two divine words —not human words at all? Has not God consecrated the state of matrimony to such an excellent mystery, that in it is signified and represented the mystical union between Christ and his Church? Are not husbands to love their wives, and give themselves for them as Christ loved the Church and gave himself for it? That, indeed, was not revealed in the Old Testament, but it is revealed in the New; and marriage, like all other human ties, is holy and divine, and comes from God down to men.

Yes. These family ties are of God. It was to show us how sacred, how Godlike they are —how eternal and necessary for all mankind— that Joseph's story was written in Holy Scripture.

They are of God, I say. And he who despises them, despises not man but God; who hath also given us his Holy Spirit to make us know how sacred these bonds are.

He who looks lightly on the love of child to parent, or brother to brother, or husband to wife, and bids each man please himself, each man help himself, and shift for himself, would take away from men the very thing which raises them above the beasts which perish, and lower them again to the likeness of the flesh, that they may of the flesh reap corruption.

They who, under whatever pretence of religion, part asunder families; or tell children, like the wicked Pharisees of old, that they may say to their parents, Corban—'I have given to God the service and help which, as your child, I should have given to you'—shall be called, if not by men, at least by God himself, hypocrites, who draw near to God with their mouths, and honour him with their lips, while their heart is far from him.

I think now we may see that I was right when I said—Perhaps the history of Joseph is in the Bible because it *is* a family history. For see, it is the history of a man who loved his family, who felt that family life was holy and God-appointed; whom God rewarded with honour and wealth, because he honoured family ties; because he refused his master's wife; because he rewarded his brothers good for evil; because he was not ashamed of his father, but succoured him in his old age.

It is the history of a man who—more than four hundred years before God gave the ten commandments on Sinai, saying,

Honour thy father and mother,

Thou shalt not commit adultery,

Thou shalt not kill in revenge,

Thou shalt not covet aught of thy neighbours
—It is the history, I say, of a man who had those laws of God written in his heart by the Holy Spirit of God; and felt that to break them

was to sin against God. It is the history of a man who, sorely tempted and unjustly persecuted, kept himself pure and true; who, while all around him, beginning with his own brothers, were trampling under foot the laws of family, felt that the laws were still there round him, girding him in with everlasting bands, and saying to him, Thou shalt and Thou shalt not; that he was not sent into the world to do just what was pleasant for the moment, to indulge his own passions or his own revenge; but that if he was indeed *a man*, he must prove himself a man, by obeying Almighty God. It is the history of a man who kept his heart pure and tender, and who thereby gained strange and deep wisdom; that wisdom which comes only to the pure in heart; that wisdom by which truly good men are enabled to see farther, and to be of more use to their fellow-creatures than many a cunning and crooked politician, whose eyes are blinded, because his heart is defiled with sin.

And now, my friends, if we pray—as we are bound to pray—for that great Prince who is just entering on the cares and the duties, as well as the joys and blessings of family life—what better prayer can we offer up for him, than that God would put into his heart that spirit which he put into the heart of Joseph of old—the spirit to see how divine and God-appointed is family life? God grant that that spirit may dwell in him, and possess him more and more day by day. That it may keep him true to his wife, true to his mother, true to his family, true, like Joseph, to all with whom he has to deal. That it may deliver him, as it delivered Joseph, from the snares of wicked women, from selfish politicians, if they ever try to sow distrust and opposition between him and his kindred, and from all those temptations which can only be kept down by the Spirit of God working in men's hearts, as he worked in the heart of Joseph.

For if that spirit be in the Prince—and I doubt not that that spirit is in him already—then will his fate be that of Joseph; then will he indeed be a blessing to us, and to our children after us; then will he have riches more real, and power more vast, than any which our English laws can give; then will he gain, like Joseph, that *moral* wisdom, better than all worldly craft, which cometh from above—first pure, then gentle, easy to be entreated, without partiality, and without hypocrisy; then will he be able, like Joseph, to deliver his people in times of perplexity and distress; then will he by his example, as his noble mother has done before him, keep healthy, pure, and strong, our English family life—and as long as *that* endures, Old England will endure likewise.

SERMON VIII.

THE BIBLE THE GREAT CIVILIZER.

(Fourth Sunday in Lent.)

PHILLIPPIANS iv. 8.

Finally, brethren, whatsoever things are true, whatsoever things
are honest, whatsoever things are just, whatsoever things are
pure, whatsoever things are lovely, whatsoever things are of
good report; if there be any virtue, and if there be any praise,
think on these things.

IT may not be easy to see what this text has
to do with the story of Joseph, which we have
just been reading, or with the meaning of the
Bible of which I have been speaking to you of
late.

Nevertheless, I think it has to do with them; as
you will see if you will look at the text with me.

Now the text does not say 'Do these things.'
It only says '*think* of these things.'

Of course St. Paul wished us to do them also:
but he says first *think* of them; not once in a way,

but often and continually. Fill your mind with good and pure and noble thoughts; and then you will do good and pure and noble things.

For out of the abundance of a man's heart, not only does his mouth speak, but his whole body and soul behave. The man whose mind is filled with low and bad thoughts will be sure, when he is tempted, to do low and bad things. The man whose mind is filled with lofty and good thoughts will do lofty and good things.

For thoughts are the food of a man's mind; and as the mind feeds, so will it grow. If it feeds on coarse and foul food, coarse and foul it will grow. If it feeds on pure and refined food, pure and refined it will grow.

There are those who do not believe this. Provided they are tolerably attentive to the duties of religion, it does not matter much, they fancy, what they think of out of church. Their souls will be saved at last, they suppose, and that is all that they need care for. Saved? They do not see that by giving way to foul, mean, foolish thoughts all the week they are losing their souls, destroying their souls, defiling their souls, lowering their souls, and making them so coarse and mean and poor that they are not worth saving, and are no loss to heaven or earth, whatever loss they may be to the man himself. One man thinks of nothing but money—how he shall save a penny here and a penny there. I do not mean men of business; for them there are great excuses; for it is by continual saving here and there that their profits are made. I speak rather of people who have no excuse, people of fixed incomes—people often wealthy and comfortable, who yet will lower their minds by continually thinking over their money. But this I say, and this I am sure that you will find, that when a man in business or out of business accustoms himself, as very many do, to think of nothing but money, money, money from Monday morning to Saturday night, he thinks of money a great part of Sunday likewise. And so, after a while, the man lowers his soul, and makes it mean and covetous. He forgets all that is lovely and of good report. He forgets virtue—that is manliness; and praise—that is the just respect and admiration of his fellow-men; and so he forgets at last things true, honest, and just likewise. He lowers his soul; and therefore when he is tempted, he does things mean and false and unjust, for the sake of money, which he has made his idol.

Take another case, too common among men and women of all ranks, high and low.

How many there are who love gossip and scandal; who always talk about people, and never about things—certainly not about things pure and lovely and of good report, but rather about things foul and ugly and of bad report; who do not talk, because they do not think of virtue, but of vice; or of praise either, because they are always finding fault with their neighbours. The man who loves a foul story, or a coarse jest—the woman who gossips over every tittle tattle of scandal which she can pick up against her neighbour— what do these people do but defile their own souls afresh, after they have been washed clean in the blood of Christ? Foul their souls are, and therefore their thoughts are foul likewise, and the foulness of them is evident to all men by their tongues. Out of their hearts proceed evil thoughts about their neighbours, out of the abundance of their hearts their mouths speak them.

Now let such people, if there be any such here, seriously consider the harm which they are doing to their own characters. They may give way to the habits of scandal, or of coarse talk, without any serious bad intention; but they will surely lower their own souls thereby. They will grow to the colour of what they feed on and become foul and cruel, from talking cruelly and foully, till they lose all purity and all charity, all faith and trust in their fellow-men, all power of seeing good in any one, or doing anything but think evil ; and so lose the likeness of God and of Christ, for the likeness of some foul carrion bird, which cares nothing for the perfume of all the roses in the world, but if there be a carcase within miles of it, will scent it out eagerly and fly to it ravenously.

The truth is, my friends, that these souls of ours, instead of being pure and strong, are the very opposite; and the article speaks plain truth when it says, that we are every one of us of our own nature inclined to evil. That may seem a hard saying ; but if we look at our own thoughts we shall find it true. Are we *not* inclined to take, at first, the worst view of everybody and of everything? Are we *not* inclined to suspect harm of this person and of that ? Are we *not* inclined too often to be mean and cowardly ? to be hard and covetous ? to be coarse and vulgar ? to be silly and frivolous ? Do we not need to cool down, to think a second time, and a third time likewise ; to remember our duty, to remember Christ's example, before we can take a just and kind and charitable view? Do we not want all the help which we can get from every quarter, to keep ourselves high-minded and refined; to keep ourselves from bad thoughts, mean thoughts, silly thoughts, violent thoughts, cruel and hard thoughts? If we have not found out that, we must have looked a very little way into ourselves, and know little more about ourselves than a dumb animal does of itself.

How then shall we keep off coarseness of soul? How shall we keep our souls *refined?* that is, true and honest, pure, amiable, full of virtue, that is, true manliness; and deserve praise, that is, the respect and admiration of our fellow-men? By thinking of those very things, says St. Paul. And in order to be able to think of them, by reading of them.

There are very few who can easily think of these things of themselves. Their daily business, the words and notions of the people with whom they have to do, will run in their minds, and draw them off from higher and better thoughts; that cannot be helped. The only thing that most men can do, is to take care that they are not drawn off entirely from high and good thoughts, by reading, were it but for five minutes every day, something really worth thinking of, something which will lift them above themselves.

Above all, it is wise, at night, after the care and bustle of the day is over, to read, but for a few minutes, some book which will compose and soothe the mind; which will bring us face to face with the true facts of life, death, and eternity; which will make us remember that man doth not live by bread alone; which will give us, before we sleep, a few thoughts worthy of a Christian man, with an immortal soul in him.

And, thank God, no one need go far to look for such books. I do not mean merely religious books, excellent as they are in these days: I mean any books which help to make us better and wiser and soberer, and more charitable persons; any books which will teach us to despise what is vulgar and mean, foul and cruel, and to love what is noble and high-minded, pure and just. We need not go far for 'them. In our own noble English language we may read by hundreds, books which will tell us of all virtue and of all praise. The stories of good and brave men and women ; of gallant and heroic actions ; of deeds which we ourselves should be proud of doing ; of persons whom we feel to be better, wiser, nobler than we are ourselves.

In our own language we may read the history of our own nation, and whatsoever is just, honest and true. We may read of God's gracious providences toward this land. How he has punished our sins and rewarded our right and brave endeavours. How he put into our forefathers the spirit of courage and freedom, the spirit of truth and justice, the spirit of loyalty and order; and how, following the leading of that spirit, in spite of many mistakes and failings, we have risen to be the freest, the happiest, the most powerful people on earth, a blessing and not a curse to the nations around.

In our own English tongue, too, we may read such poetry as there is in no other language in the world ; poetry which will make us indeed see the beauty of whatsoever things are lovely and of good report. Some people have still a dislike of what they call foolish poetry books. If books are foolish, let us have nothing to do with them. But poetry ought not to be foolish ; for God sent it into the world to teach men not foolishness, but the highest wisdom. He gave man alone, of all living creatures, the power of writing poetry, that by poetry he might understand, not only how necessary it was to do right, but how beautiful and noble it was to do right. He sent it into the world to soften men's rough hearts, and quiet their angry passions, and make them love all which is tender and gentle, loving and merciful, and yet to rouse them up to love all which is gallant and honourable, loyal and patriotic, devout and heavenly. Therefore whole books of the Bible—Job, for example, Isaiah, and the Psalms—are neither more nor less than actual poetry, written in actual verse, that their words might the better sink down into the ears and hearts of the old Jews, and of us Christians after them. And therefore also, we keep up still the good old custom of teaching children in school as much as possible by poetry, that they may learn not only to know, but to love and remember whatsoever things are lovely and of good report.

Lastly, for those who cannot read, or have really no time to read, there is one means left of putting themselves in mind of what every one must remember, lest he sink back into an animal and a savage. I mean by pictures; which, as St. Augustine said 1400 years ago, are the books of the unlearned. I do not mean grand and expensive pictures; I mean the very simplest prints, provided they represent something holy, or noble, or tender, or lovely. A few such prints upon a cottage-wall may teach the people who live therein much, without their being aware of it. They see the prints, even when they are not thinking of them; and so they have before their eyes a continual remembrancer of something better and more beautiful than what they are apt to find in their own daily life and thoughts.

True, to whom little is given, of them is little required. But it must be said, that more—far more—is given to labouring men and women now than was given to their forefathers. A hundred, or even fifty years ago, when there was very little schooling; when the books which were put even into the hands of noblemen's children were far below what you will find now in any village school; when the only pictures which a poor woman could buy to lay on her cottage-wall were equally silly and ugly: then there were great excuses for the poor, if they forgot whatsoever things were lovely and of good report; if they were often coarse and brutal in their manners, and cruel and profligate in their amusements.

But even in the rough old times there always were a few at least, men and women, who were *above* the rest; who, though poor people like the rest, were still true gentlemen and ladies of God's making. People who kept themselves more or less unspotted from the world; who thought of what was honest and pure and lovely and of good report; and who lived a life of simple, manful, Christian virtue, and received the praise and respect of their neighbours, even although their neighbours did not copy them. There were always such people, and there always will be—thank God for it, for they are the salt of the earth.

But why have there always been such people? and why do I say confidently, that there always will be?

Because they have had the Bible; and because, once having got the Bible in a free country, no man can take it from them.

The Bible it is which has made gentlemen and ladies of many a poor man and woman.

The Bible it is which has filled their minds with pure and noble, ay, with heavenly and divine thoughts.

The Bible has been their whole library. The Bible has been their only counsellor. The Bible has taught them all they know. But it has taught them enough.

It has taught them what God is, and what

Christ is. It has taught them what man is, and what a Christian man should be. It has taught them what a family means, and what a nation means. It has taught them the meaning of law and duty, of loyalty and patriotism. It has filled their minds with things honest and just and lovely and of good report; with the histories of men and women like themselves, who sinned and sorrowed and struggled like them in this hard battle of life, but who conquered at last, by trusting and obeying God.

This one story of Joseph, which we have been reading again this Sunday, I do not doubt that it has taught thousands who had no other story-book to read—who could not even read themselves, but had to listen to others' reading; that it has taught them to be good sons, to be good brothers; that it has taught them to keep pure in temptation, and patient and honest under oppression and wrong; that it has stirred in them a noble ambition to raise themselves in life; and taught them, at the same time, that the only safe and sure way of rising is to fear God and keep his commandments; and so has really done more to civilize and refine them—to make them truly civilized men and gentlemen, and not vulgar savages—than if they had known a smattering of a dozen sciences. I say that the Bible is the book which civilizes and refines, and ennobles rich and poor, high and low, and has been doing so for fifteen hundred years; and that any man who tries to shake our faith in the Bible, is doing what he can—though, thank God, he will not succeed—to make such rough and coarse heathens of us again as our forefathers were five hundred years ago.

And I tell you, labouring people, that if you want something which will make up to you for the want of all the advantages which the rich have—go to your Bibles and you will find it there.

There you will find, in the history of men like ourselves—and, above all, in the history of a man unlike ourselves, the perfect Man—perfect Man and perfect God together—whatsoever is true, whatsoever is honest, just, pure, lovely, and of good report; every virtue, and every just cause of praise which mortal man can desire. Read of them in your Bible, think of them in your hearts, feed on them with your souls, that your souls may grow like what they feed on; and above all, read and study the story and character of Jesus Christ himself, our Lord, that beholding, as in a glass, the glory of the Lord, you may be changed into his likeness, from grace to grace, and virtue to virtue, and glory to glory.

And that change and that growth are as easy for the poor as for the rich, and as necessary for the rich as for the poor.

SERMON IX.

MOSES.

(Fifth Sunday in Lent.)

Exodus iii. 14.

And God said unto Moses, I AM THAT I AM.

AND now, my friends, we are come, on this Sunday, to the most beautiful, and the most important story of the whole Bible—excepting of course, the story of our Lord Jesus Christ—the story of how a family grew to be a great nation. You remember that I told you that the history of the Jews, had been only, as yet, the history of a family.

Now that family is grown to be a great tribe, a great herd of people, but not yet a *nation;* one people, with its own God, its own worship, its own laws; but such a mere tribe, or band of tribes as the gipsies are among us now; a herd, but not a nation.

Then the Bible tells us how these tribes, being weak I suppose because they had no laws, nor patriotism, nor fellow-feeling of their own, became slaves, and suffered for hundreds of years under crafty kings and cruel taskmasters.

Then it tells us how God delivered them out of their slavery, and made them free men. And how God did that (for God in general works by means), by the means of a man, a prophet and a hero, one great, wise, and good man of their race—Moses.

It tells us, too, how God trained Moses, by a very strange education, to be the fit man to deliver his people.

Let us go through the history of Moses; and we shall see how God trained him to do the work for which God wanted him.

Let us read from the account of the Bible itself. I should be sorry to spoil its noble simplicity by any words of my own: 'And the children of Israel were fruitful, and increased abundantly, and multiplied, and waxed exceeding mighty; and the land was filled with them. Now there arose up a new king over Egypt, which knew not Joseph. And he said unto his people, Behold, the people of the children of

Israel are more and mightier than we: Come on, let us deal wisely with them; lest they multiply, and it come to pass, that, when there falleth out any war, they join also unto our enemies, and fight against us, and so get them up out of the land. Therefore they did set over them taskmasters to afflict them with their burdens. And they built for Pharaoh treasure cities, Pithon and Raamses. . . . And Pharaoh charged all his people, saying, Every son that is born ye shall cast into the river, and every daughter ye shall save alive. And there went a man of the house of Levi, and took to wife a daughter of Levi. And the woman conceived and bare a son: and when she saw him that he was a goodly child, she hid him three months. And when she could no longer hide him, she took for him an ark of bulrushes, and daubed it with slime and with pitch, and put the child therein: and she laid it in the flags by the river's brink. And his sister stood afar off, to wit what would be done to him. And the daughter of Pharaoh came down to wash herself at the river; and her maidens walked along by the river's side; and when she saw the ark among the flags, she sent her maid to fetch it. And when she had opened

it, she saw the child; and behold the babe wept.
And she had compassion on him, and said, This
is one of the Hebrews' children. Then said his
sister to Pharaoh's daughter, Shall I go and call to
thee a nurse of the Hebrew women, that she may
nurse the child for thee? And Pharaoh's daughter
said to her, Go. And the maid went and called
the child's mother. And Pharaoh's daughter said
unto her, Take this child away, and nurse it for
me, and I will give thee thy wages. And the
woman took the child, and nursed it. And the
child grew, and she brought him unto Pharaoh's
daughter, and he became her son. And she called
his name Moses: and she said, Because I drew
him out of the water.'

Moses, the child of the water. St. Paul in
the Epistle to the Hebrews says that Moses was
called the son of Pharaoh's daughter; that is,
adopted by her. We read elsewhere that he was
learned in all the wisdom of the Egyptians, of
which there can be no doubt from his own writings,
especially that part called Moses' law.

So that Moses had from his youth vast advantages. Brought up in the court of the greatest
king of the world, in one of the greatest cities
of the world, among the most learned priesthood

in the world, he had learned, probably, all statesmanship, all religion, which man could teach him in those old times.

But that would have been little for him. He might have become merely an officer in Pharaoh's household, and we might never have heard his name, and he might never have done any good to his own people and to all mankind after them, as he has done, if there had not been something better and nobler in him than all the learning and statesmanship of the Egyptians.

For there was in Moses the spirit of God; the spirit which makes a man believe in God, and trust God. 'And therefore,' says St. Paul, 'he refused to be called the son of Pharaoh's daughter; esteeming the reproach of *Christ* better than all the treasures in Egypt.'

And how did he do that? In this wise.

The spirit of God and of Christ is also the spirit of justice, the spirit of freedom; the spirit which hates oppression and wrong; which is moved with a noble and Divine indignation at seeing any human being abused and trampled on.

And that spirit broke forth in Moses. 'And it came to pass in those days, when Moses was grown, that he went out unto his brethren, and looked on their burdens : and he spied an Egyptian smiting an Hebrew, one of his brethren. And he looked this way and that way, and when he saw that there was no man, he slew the Egyptian, and hid him in the sand.'

If he cannot get justice for his people, he will do some sort of rough justice for them himself, when he has an opportunity.

But he will see fair play among his people themselves. They are, as slaves are likely to be, fallen and base ; unjust and quarrelsome among themselves.

' And when he went out the second day, behold, two men of the Hebrews strove together : and he said to him that did the wrong, Wherefore smitest thou thy fellow ? And he said, Who made thee a prince and a judge over us ? intendest thou to kill me as thou killedst the Egyptian ? And Moses feared, and said,' Surely this thing is known. Now when Pharaoh heard this thing, he sought to slay Moses. But Moses fled from the face of Pharaoh, and dwelt in the land of Midian'—the wild desert between Egypt and the Holy Land.

So he bore the reproach of Christ ; the reproach which is apt to fall on men in bad times, when they try, like our Lord Jesus Christ, to deliver the captive, and let the oppressed go free, and execute righteous judgment in the earth. He had lost all, by trying to do right. He had been powerful and honoured in Pharaoh's court. Now he was an outcast and wanderer in the desert. He had made his first trial, and failed. As St. Stephen said of him after, he supposed that his brethren would have understood how God would deliver them by his hand; but they understood not. Slavish, base, and stupid, they were not fit yet for Moses and his deliverance.

And so forty years went on, and Moses was an old man of eighty years of age. Yet God had not had mercy on his poor countrymen in Egypt.

It must have been a strange life for him, the adopted son of Pharaoh's daughter; brought up in the court of the most powerful and highly civilized country of the old world; learned in all the learning of the Egyptians; and now married into a tribe of wild Arabs, keeping flocks in the lonely desert, year after year: but, no doubt, thinking, thinking, year after year, as he fed his flocks alone. Thinking over all the learning which he had gained in Egypt, and wondering whether it would ever be of any use to him. Thinking over the misery of his people in Egypt, and wondering whether he should ever be able to help them. Thinking, too, and more than all, of God—of God's promise to Abraham and his children. Would that ever come true? Would *God* help these wretched Jews, even if *he* could not? Was God faithful and true, just and merciful?

That Moses thought of God, that he never lost faith in God for that forty years, there can be no doubt.

If he had not thought of God, God would not have revealed himself to him. If he had lost faith in God, he would not have known that it *was* God who spoke to him. If he had lost faith in God, he would not have obeyed God at the risk of his life, and have gone on an errand as desperate, dangerous, hopeless—and, humanly speaking, as wild as ever man went upon.

But Moses never lost faith or patience. He believed, and he did not make haste. He waited for God; and he did not wait in vain. No man will wait in vain. When the time was ready; when the Jews were ready; when Pharaoh was ready; when Moses himself, trained by forty years' patient thought, was ready; then God came in his own good time.

And Moses led the flock to the back of the

desert, and came to the mountain of God, even to Horeb. And there he saw a bush—probably one of the low copses of acacia—burning with fire; and behold the bush was not consumed. Then out of the bush God spoke to Moses with an audible voice as of a man; so the Bible says plainly, and I see no reason to doubt that it is literally true.

'Moreover he said, I am the God of thy father, the God of Abraham, the God of Isaac, and the God of Jacob. And Moses hid his face; for he was afraid to look upon God. And the Lord said, I have surely seen the affliction of my people which are in Egypt, and have heard their cry by reason of their taskmasters; for I know their sorrows; and I am come down to deliver them out of the hand of the Egyptians, and to bring them up out of that land unto a good land and a large, unto a land flowing with milk and honey; unto the place of the Canaanites, and the Hittites, and the Amorites, and the Perizzites, and the Hivites, and the Jebusites.'

Then followed a strange conversation. Moses was terrified at the thought of what he had to do, and reasonably: moreover, the Israelites in Egypt had forgotten God. 'And Moses said unto

God, Behold, when I come unto the children of Israel, and shall say unto them, The God of your fathers hath sent me unto you; and they shall say to me, What is his name? what shall I say unto them? And God said unto Moses, I Am that I Am: and he said, Thus shalt thou say unto the children of Israel, I Am hath sent me unto you.'

I Am; that was the new name by which God revealed himself to Moses. That message of God to Moses was the greatest Gospel, and good news which was spoken to men, before the coming of our Lord Jesus Christ. Ay, we are feeling now, in our daily life, in our laws and our liberty, our religion and our morals, our peace and prosperity, in the happiness of our homes, and I trust that of our consciences, the blessed effects of that message, which God revealed to Moses in the wilderness thousands of years ago.

And Moses took his wife, and his sons, and set them upon an ass, and returned into the land of Egypt, to say to Pharaoh, 'Thus saith the Lord, Israel is my son, even my firstborn, Let my son go that he may serve me, and if thou let not my firstborn go, then I will slay thy firstborn.'

A strange man, on a strange errand. A poor

man, eighty years old, carrying all that he had in the world upon an ass's back, going down to the great Pharaoh, the greatest king of the old world, the great conqueror, the Child of the Sun (as his name means), one of the greatest Pharaohs who ever sat on the throne of Egypt; in the midst of all his princes and priests, and armies with which he had conquered the nations far and wide; and his great cities, temples, and palaces, on which men may see at this day (so we are told) the face of that very Pharaoh painted again and again, as fresh, in that rainless air, as on the day when the paint was laid on; with the features of a man terrible, proud, and cruel, puffed up by power till he thought himself, and till his people thought him a god on earth.

And to that man was Moses going, to bid him set the children of Israel free; while he himself was one of that very slave-race of the Israelites, which was an abomination to the Egyptians, who held them all as lepers and unclean, and would not eat with them; and an outcast too, who had fled out of Egypt for his life, and who might be killed on the spot, as Pharaoh's only answer to his bold request. Certainly, if Moses had not had faith in God, his errand would have seemed that of a madman. But Moses *had* faith in God; and of faith it is said, that it can remove mountains, for all things are possible to them who believe.

So by faith Moses went back into Egypt; how he fared there we shall hear next Sunday.

And what sort of man was this great and wonderful Moses, whose name will last as long as man is man? We know very little. We know from the Bible and from the old traditions of the Jews that he was a very handsome man; a man of a noble presence, as one can well believe; a man of great bodily vigour; so that when he died at the age of one hundred and twenty, his eye was not dim, nor his natural force abated. We know, from his own words, that he was slow of speech; that he had more thought in him than he could find words for— very different from a good many loud talkers, who have more words than thoughts, and who get a great character as politicians and demagogues, simply because they have the art of stringing fine words together, which Moses, the true demagogue, the leader of the people, who led them indeed out of Egypt, had not. Beyond that we know little. Of his character one thing only is said: but that is most important. 'Now the man Moses was very meek.'

Meek: we know that that cannot mean that he was meek in the sense that he was a poor, cowardly, abject sort of man, who dared not speak his mind, dared not face the truth, and say the truth. We have seen that that was just what he was not; brave, determined, out-spoken, he seems to have been from his youth. Indeed, if his had been that base sort of meekness, he never would have dared to come before the great king Pharaoh. If he had been that sort of man he never would have dared to lead the Jews through the Red Sea by night, or out of Egypt at all. If he had been that sort of man, indeed, the Jews would never have listened to him. No; he had—the Bible tells us that he had—to say and do stern things again and again; to act like the general of an army, or the commander of a ship of war, who must be obeyed, even though men's lives be the forfeit of disobedience.

But the man Moses was very meek. He had learned to keep his temper. Indeed, the story seems to say that he never lost his temper really but once; and for that God punished him. Never man was so tried, save One, even our Lord Jesus

Christ, as was Moses. And yet by patience he conquered. Eighty years had he spent in learning to keep his temper; and when he had learned to keep his temper, then, and not till then, was he worthy to bring his people out of Egypt. That was a long schooling, but it was a schooling worth having.

And if we, my friends, spend our whole lives, be they eighty years long, in learning to keep *our* tempers, then will our lives have been well spent. For meekness and calmness of temper need not interfere with a man's courage or justice, or honest indignation against wrong, or power of helping his fellow-men. Moses' meekness did not make him a coward or a sluggard. It helped him to do his work rightly instead of wrongly; it helped him to conquer the pride of Pharaoh, and the faithlessness, cowardice, and rebellion of his brethren, those miserable slavish Jews. And so meekness, an even temper, and a gracious tongue, will help us to keep our place among our fellow-men with true dignity and independence, and to govern our households, and train our children in such a way that while they obey us they will love and respect us at the same time.

SERMON X.

THE PLAGUES OF EGYPT.

(Palm Sunday.)

Exodus ix. 13, 14.

Thus saith the Lord God of the Hebrews, Let my people go,
that they may serve me. For I will at this time send all my
plagues upon thine heart, and upon thy servants, and upon
thy people; that thou mayest know that there is none like
me in all the earth.

YOU will understand, I think, the meaning
of the ten plagues of Egypt better, if I
explain to you in a few words what kind of a
country Egypt is, what kind of people the Egyptians were. Some of you, doubtless, know as well
as I, but some here may not: it is for them I
speak.

Egypt is one of the strangest countries in the
world; and yet one which can be most simply
described. One long straight strip of rich flat land,
many hundred miles long, but only a very few

miles broad. On either side of it, barren rocks and deserts of sand, and running through it from end to end, the great river Nile—'The River' of which the Bible speaks. This river the Egyptians looked on as divine: they worshipped it as a god; for on it depended the whole wealth of Egypt. Every year it overflows the whole country, leaving behind it a rich coat of mud, which makes Egypt the most inexhaustibly fertile land in the world; and made the Egyptians, from very ancient times, the best farmers of the world, the fathers of agriculture. Meanwhile, when not in flood, the river water is of the purest in the world; the most delightful to drink; and was supposed in old times to be a cure for all manner of diseases.

To worship this sacred river, the pride of their land, to drink it, to bathe in it, to catch the fish which abound in it, and which formed then, and forms still, the staple food of the Egyptians, was their delight. And now I have told you enough to show you why the plagues which God sent on Egypt began first by striking the river.

The river, we read, was turned into blood. What that means—whether it was actual animal blood—what means God employed to work the miracle—are just the questions about which we need not trouble our minds. We never shall know: and we need not know. The plain fact is, that the sacred river, pure and life-giving, became a detestable mass of rottenness—and with it all their streams and pools, and drinking water in vessels of wood and stone—for all, remember, came from the Nile, carried by canals and dykes over the whole land. 'And the fish that were in the river died, and the river stunk, and there was blood through all the land of Egypt.'

The slightest thought will show us what horror, confusion, and actual want and misery, the loss of the river water, even for a few days or even hours, would cause.

But there is more still in this miracle. These plagues are a battle between Jehovah, the one true and only God Almighty, and the false gods of Egypt, to prove which of them is master.

Pharaoh answers: 'Who is Jehovah (the Lord) that I should let Israel go?' I know not the Jehovah. I have my own god, whom I worship. He is my father, and I his child, and he will protect me. If I obey any one it will be him.

Be it so, says Moses in the name of God. Thou shalt know that the idols of Egypt are nothing, that they cannot deliver thee nor thy people.

Thus saith Jehovah, Thou shalt know which is master, I or they. 'Thou shalt know that I am the Lord.'

So the river was turned into blood. The sacred river was no god, as they thought. Jehovah was the Lord and Master of the river on which the very life of Egypt depended. He could turn it into blood. All Egypt was at his mercy.

But Pharaoh would not believe that. 'The magicians did likewise with their enchantments' —made, we may suppose, water seem to turn to blood by some juggling trick at which the priests in Egypt were but too well practised; and Pharaoh seemed to have made up his mind that Moses' miracle was only a juggling trick too. For men will make up their minds to anything, however absurd, when they choose to do so: when their pride, and rage, and obstinacy, and covetousness, draw them one way, no reason will draw them the other way. They will find reasons, and make reasons to prove, if need be, that there is no sun in the sky.

Then followed a series of plagues, of which we have all often heard.

Learned men have disputed how far these plagues were miracles. Some of them are said not to be uncommon in Egypt, others to be almost unknown. But whether they—whether the frogs, for instance, were not produced by natural causes, just as other frogs are ; and the lice and the flies likewise ; that I know not, my friends, neither need I know. If they were not, they were miraculous ; and if they were, they were miraculous still. If they came as other vermin come, they would have still been miraculous : God would still have sent them ; and it would be a miracle that God should make them come at that particular time in that particular country, to work a truly miraculous effect upon the souls of Pharaoh and the Egyptians on the one hand, and of Moses and the Israelites on the other. But if they came by some strange means as no vermin ever came before or since, all I can say is—Why not ?

And the Lord said unto Moses, 'Say unto Aaron, Stretch out thy rod and smite the dust of the land, that it may become lice throughout all the land of Egypt.'

Whether that was meant only as a sign to the Egyptians, or whether the dust did literally turn into lice, we do not know, and what is more, we need not know; if God chose that it should be so, so it would be. If you believe at all that God made the world, it is folly to pretend to set any bounds to his power. As a wise man has said, 'If you believe in any real God at all, you must believe that miracles can happen.' He makes you and me and millions of living things out of the dust of the ground continually by certain means. Why can he not make lice, or anything else out of the dust of the ground, without those means? I can give no reason, nor any one else either.

We know that God has given all things a law which they cannot break. We know, too, that God will never break his own laws. But what are God's laws by which he makes things? We do not know.

Miracles may be—indeed must be—only the effect of some higher and deeper laws of God. We cannot prove that he breaks his law, or disturbs his order by them. They may seem contrary to some of the very very few laws of God's earth which we do know. But they need not be contrary to the very many laws which we do not know. In fact, we know nothing about the matter, and had best not talk of things that we do not understand. As for these things being too wonderful to be true—that is an argument which only deserves a smile. There are so many wonders in the world round us already, all day long, that the man of sense will feel that nothing is too wonderful to be true.

The truth is, that, as a wise man says, *Custom* is the great enemy of Faith, and of Reason likewise; and one of the worst tricks which custom plays us is, making us fancy that miraculous things cease to be miraculous by becoming common.

What do I mean?

This: which every child in this church can understand.

You think it very wonderful that God should cause frogs to come upon the whole land of Egypt in one day. But that God should cause frogs to come up every spring in the ditches does not seem wonderful to you at all. It happens every year; therefore, forsooth, there is nothing wonderful in it.

Ah, my dear friends, it is custom which blinds our eyes to the wisdom of God, and the wonders of God, and the power of God, and the glory of God, and hinders us from believing the message with which he speaks to us from every sunbeam and every shower, every blade of grass and every standing pool. 'Is anything too hard for the Lord?'

If any man here says that anything is too hard for the Lord, let him go this day to the nearest standing pool, and look at the frog-spawn therein, and consider it till he confesses his blindness and foolishness. That spawn seems to you a foul thing, the produce of mean, ugly, contemptible creatures. Be it so. Yet it is to the eyes of the wise man a yearly *miracle;* a thing past understanding, past explaining; one which will make him feel the truth of that great 139th Psalm: 'Thou hast beset me behind and before, and laid thine hand upon me. Such knowledge is too wonderful for me; it is high, I cannot attain unto it. Whither shall I go from thy spirit? or whither shall I flee from thy presence? If I ascend up into heaven, thou art there: if I make my bed in hell, behold, thou art there also.'

That every one of those little black spots should have in it *life*—What is life? How did it get into that black spot? or, to speak more carefully, is the life *in* the black spot at all? Is not the life in the Spirit of God, who is working on that spot, as I believe? How has that black spot the power of *growing*, and of growing on a certain and fixed plan, merely by the quickening power of the sun's heat, and then of feeding itself, and of changing its shape, as you all know, again and again, till—and if that is not wonderful, what is?—it turns into a frog, exactly like its parent, utterly unlike the black dot at which it began? Is that no miracle? Is it no miracle that not one of those black spots ever turns into anything save a frog? Why should not some of them turn into toads or efts? Why not even into fishes or serpents? Why not? The eggs of all those animals, in their first and earliest stages are exactly alike; the microscope shows no difference. Ay, even the mere animal and the human being, strange and awful as it may be, *seem*, under the microscope, to have the same beginning. And yet one becomes a mere animal, and the other a member of Christ, a child of God, and an inheritor of the kingdom of heaven. What causes this but the power of God, making of the same clay one vessel to honour and another to dishonour? And yet people will not believe in miracles! Why does each kind turn into its kind? Answer that. Because it is a law of nature? Not so! There are no laws *of* nature. God is a law *to* nature. It is his *will* that things so should be ; and when it is his will they will not be so, but otherwise.

Not *laws* of nature, but the *Spirit* of God, as the Psalms truly say, gives life and breath to all things. Of him and by him is all. As the greatest chemist of our time says, 'Causes are the acts of God—creation is the will of God.'

And he that is wise and strong enough to create frogs in one way in every ditch at this moment, is he not wise and strong enough to create frogs by some other way, if he should choose, whether in Egypt of old, or now, here, this very day ?

Whatsoever means, or no means at all, God used to produce those vermin, the miracle remains the same. He sent them to do a work, and they did it. He sent them to teach Egyptian and Israelite alike that he was the Maker, and Lord, and Ruler of the world, and all that therein is ; that he would have his way, and that he *could* have his way.

Intensely painful and disgusting these plagues must have been to the Egyptians, for this reason, that they were the most cleanly of all people. They had a dislike of dirt, which had become quite a superstition to them. Their priests (magicians as the Bible calls them) never wore any garments but linen, for fear of their harbouring vermin of any kind. And this extreme cleanliness of theirs the next plague struck at; they were covered with boils and diseases of skin, and the magicians could not stand before Pharaoh by reason of the boils. They became unclean and unfit for their office; they could perform no religious ceremonies, and had to flee away in disgrace.

After plagues of thunder, hail, and rain, which seldom or never happen in that rainless land of Egypt; after a plague of locusts, which are very rare there, and have to come many hundred miles if they come at all; of darkness, seemingly impossible in a land where the sun always shines: then came the last and most terrible plague of all. After solemn warnings of what was coming, the angel of the Lord passed through the land of Egypt, and smote all the first-born in Egypt, from the first-born of Pharaoh upon his throne to the first-born of the captive in the dungeon; and there arose a great cry in Egypt, for there was not a house in which there was not one dead. A terrible and heart-rending calamity in any case, enough to break the heart of all Egypt; and it did break the heart of Egypt, and the proud heart of Pharaoh himself, and they let the people go.

But this was a *religious* affliction too. Most of these first-born children—probably all the first-born of the priests and nobles, and of Pharaoh himself—were consecrated to some god. They bore the name of the god to whom they belonged; that god was to prosper and protect them, and behold, he could not. The Lord Jehovah, the God of the Hebrews, was stronger than all the gods of Egypt; none of them could deliver their servants out of his hand. He was the only Lord of life and death; he had given them life, and he could take it away, in spite of all and every one of the gods of the Egyptians.

So the Lord God showed himself to be the Master and Lord of all things. The Lord of the sacred river Nile; the Lord of the meanest vermin which crept on the earth; the Lord of the weather—able to bring thunder and hail into a land where thunder and hail was never seen before; the Lord of the locust swarms—able to bring them over the desert and over the sea to devour up every green thing in the land, and then to send a wind off the Mediterranean Sea, and drive the locusts away to the eastward; the Lord of light—who could darken, even in that cloudless land, the very sun, whom Pharaoh worshipped as his god and his ancestor ; and lastly, the Lord of human life and death—able to kill whom he chose, when he chose, and as he chose. The Lord of the earth and all that therein is ; before whom all men, even proud Pharaoh, must bow and confess, 'Is anything too hard for the Lord?'

And now, I always tell you that each fresh portion of the Old Testament reveals to men something fresh concerning the character of God. You may say, These plagues of Egypt reveal God's mighty power, but what do they reveal of his character? They reveal this : that there is in God that which, for want of a better word, we must call anger; a quite awful sternness and severity ; not only a power to punish, but a determination to punish, if men will not take his warnings—if men will not obey his will.

There is no use trying to hide from ourselves that awful truth—God is not weakly indulgent. Our God can be, if he will, a consuming fire. Upon the sinner he will surely rain fire and brimstone, storm and tempest of some kind or other. This shall be their portion too surely. Vengeance is his, and vengeance he will take. But upon whom? On the proud and the tyrannical, on the cruel, the false, the unjust. So say the Psalms again and again, and so says the history of these plagues of Egypt. Therefore his anger is a loving anger, a just anger, a merciful anger, a useful anger, an anger exercised for the good of mankind. See in this case why did God destroy the crops of Egypt—even the first-born of Egypt? Merely for the pleasure of destroying? God forbid. It was to deliver the poor Israelites from their cruel taskmasters; to force these Egyptians by terrible lessons, since they were deaf to the voice of justice and humanity—to force them, I say—to have mercy on their fellow-creatures, and let the oppressed go free. Therefore God was, even in Egypt, a God of love, who desired the good of man, who would do justice for those who were unjustly treated, even though it cost his love a pang; for none can believe that God is pleased at having to punish, pleased at having to destroy the works of his own hands, or the creatures which he has made. No; the Lord was a God of love even when he sent his sore plagues on Egypt, and therefore we may believe what the Bible tells us, that that same Lord showed, as on this day, a still greater proof of his love, when, as on this day, he entered into Jerusalem, meek and lowly, sitting on an ass, and going, as he well knew, to certain death. Before the week was over he would be betrayed, mocked, scourged, crucified by the very people whom he came to save; and yet he did it, he endured it. Instead of pouring out on them, as on the Egyptians of old, the cup of wrath and misery, he put out his hand, took the cup of wrath and misery to himself, and drank it to its very dregs. Was not that, too, a miracle? Ay, a greater miracle than all the plagues of Egypt. They were physical miracles; this a moral miracle. They were miracles of nature; this of grace. They were miracles of the Lord's power; these of the Lord's love. Think of that miracle of miracles which was worked in this Passion Week—the miracle of the Lord Jehovah stooping to die for sinful man, and say after that there is anything too hard for the Lord.

SERMON XI.

THE GOD OF THE OLD TESTAMENT IS THE GOD OF THE NEW.

(Palm Sunday.)

EXODUS ix. 14.

I will at this time send all my plagues upon thine heart, and upon thy servants, and upon thy people, that thou mayest know that there is none like me in all the earth.

WE are now beginning Passion Week, the week of the whole year which ought to teach us most theology; that is, most concerning God, his character and his spirit.

For in this Passion Week God did that which utterly and perfectly showed forth his glory, as it never has been shown forth before or since. In this week Jesus Christ, the incarnate God, died on the cross for man, and showed that his name, his character, his glory was love—love without bound or end.

It was to teach us this that the special services, lessons, collects, epistles, and gospels of this week were chosen.

The second lesson, the collects, the epistles, the gospel for to-day, all set before us the patience of Christ, the humility of Christ, the love of Christ, the self-sacrifice of Christ, the Lamb without spot, enduring all things that he might save sinful man.

But if so, what does this first lesson—the chapter of Exodus from which my text is taken— what does it teach us concerning God? Does it teach us that his name is love?

At first sight you would think that it did not. At first sight you would fancy that it spoke of God in quite a different tone from the second lesson.

In the second lesson, the words of Jesus the Son of God are all gentleness, patience, tenderness. A quiet sadness hangs over them all. They are the words of one who is come (as he said himself), not to destroy men's lives, but to save them ; not to punish sins, but to wash them away by his own most precious blood.

But in the first lesson how differently he seems to speak. His words there are the words of a stern and awful judge, who can, and who will destroy whatsoever interferes with his will and his purpose.

'I will at this time send all my plagues upon thine heart, and on thy servants, and all thy people, that thou mayest know that there is none like me in all the earth.' The cattle and sheep shall be destroyed with murrain; man and beast shall be tormented with boils and blains; the crops shall be smitten with hail; the locusts shall eat up every green thing in the land; and at last all the first-born of Egypt shall die in one night, and the land be filled with mourning, horror, and desolation, before the anger of this terrible God, who will destroy and destroy till he makes himself obeyed.

Can this be he who rode into Jerusalem, as on this day, meek and lowly, upon an ass's colt; who on the night that he was betrayed washed his disciples' feet, even the feet of Judas who betrayed him? Who prayed for his murderers as he hung upon the cross, 'Father, forgive them, for they know not what they do?'

Can these two be the same?

Is the Lord Jehovah of the Old Testament the Lord Jesus of the New?

They are the same, my friends. He who laid

waste the land of Egypt is he who came to seek and to save that which was lost.

He who slew the children in Egypt is he who took little children up in his arms and blessed them.

He who spoke the awful words of the text is he who was brought as a lamb to the slaughter; and as a sheep before the shearers is dumb, so he opened not his mouth.

This is very wonderful. But why should it *not* be wonderful? What can God be but wonderful? His character, just because it is perfect, must contain in itself all other characters, all forms of spiritual life which are without sin. And yet again it is not so very wonderful. Have we not seen—I have often—in the same mortal man these two different characters at once? Have we not seen soldiers and sailors, brave men, stern men, men who have fought in many a bloody battle, to whom it is a light thing to kill their fellow-men, or to be killed themselves in the cause of duty; and yet most full of tenderness, as gentle as lambs to little children and to weak women; nursing the sick lovingly and carefully with the same hand which would not shrink from firing the fatal cannon to blast a whole company into eternity, or sink a ship with all its crew? I have seen such men, brave as the lion and gentle as the lamb, and I saw in them the likeness of Christ—the Lion of Judah; and yet the Lamb of God.

Christ is the Lamb of God; and in him there are the innocence of the lamb, the gentleness of the lamb, the patience of the lamb: but there is more. What words are these which St. John speaks in the spirit?—

'And the heaven departed as a scroll when it is rolled together, and every mountain and island were moved out of their places; and the kings of the earth, and the great, and the rich, and the chief captains, and the mighty men, and every bondman and every freeman hid themselves in the dens and in the rocks of the mountains; and said to the mountains and to the rocks, Fall on us, and hide us from the face of him that sitteth on the throne, and from the wrath of the Lamb; for the great day of his wrath is come; and who shall be able to stand?'

Yes, look at that awful book of Revelation with which the Bible ends, and see if the Bible does not end as it began, by revealing a God who, however loving and merciful, long-suffering, and of great goodness, still wages war eternally against all sin and unrighteousness of man, and who will by no means clear the guilty; a God of whom the apostle St. Paul, who knew most of his mercy and forgiveness to sinners, could nevertheless say, just as Moses had said ages before him, 'Our God is a consuming fire.'

Now I think it most necessary to recollect this in Passion Week; ay, and to do more—to remember it all our lives long.

For it is too much the fashion now, and has often been so before, to think only of one side of our Lord's character, of the side which seems more pleasant and less awful. People please themselves in hymns which talk of the meek and lowly Jesus, and in pictures which represent him with a sad, weary, delicate, almost feminine face. Now I do not say that this is wrong. He is the same yesterday, to-day, and for ever; as tender, as compassionate now as when he was on earth ; and it is good that little children and innocent young people should think of him as an altogether gentle, gracious, loveable being; for with the meek he will be meek ; but again, with the froward, the violent, and self-willed, he will be froward. He will show the violent that he is the stronger of the two, and the self-willed that he will have his will and not theirs done.

So it is good that the widow and the orphan, the weary and the distressed, should think of Jesus as utterly tender and true, compassionate and merciful, and rest their broken hearts upon him, the everlasting rock. But while it is written, that whosoever shall fall on that rock he shall be broken, it is written too, that on whomsoever that rock shall fall, it will grind him to powder.

It is good that those who wish to be gracious themselves, loving themselves, should remember that Christ is gracious, Christ is loving. But it is good also, that those who do *not* wish to be gracious and loving themselves, but to be proud and self-willed, unjust and cruel, should remember that the gracious and loving Christ is also the most terrible and awful of all beings; sharper than a two-edged sword, piercing asunder the very joints and marrow, discerning the most secret thoughts and intents of the heart; a righteous judge, strong and patient, who is provoked every day: but if a man *will* not turn he will whet his sword. He hath bent his bow and made it ready, and laid his arrows in order against the persecutors. What Christ's countenance, my friends, was like when on earth, we do *not* know; but what his countenance is like now, we all may know; for what says

St. John, and how did Christ appear to him, who had been on earth his private and beloved friend ?

'His head and his hair were white as snow, and his eyes were like a flame of fire, and his voice like the sound of many waters; and out of his mouth went a sharp two-edged sword, and his countenance was as the sun when he shineth in his strength. And when I saw him, I fell at his feet as dead.'

That is the likeness of Christ, my friends; and we must remember that it is his likeness, and fall at his feet, and humble ourselves before his unspeakable majesty, if we wish that he should do to us at the last day as he did to St. John—lay his hand upon us, saying, 'Fear not, I am the first and the last, and behold, I am alive for evermore, Amen. I have the keys of death and hell.'

Yes, it is good that we should all remember this. For if we do not, we may fall, as thousands fall, into a very unwholesome and immoral notion about religion. We may get to fancy, as thousands do, rich and poor, that because Christ the Lord is meek and gentle, patient and long-suffering, that he is therefore easy, indulgent, careless about our doing wrong; and that we can, in plain English, trifle with Christ, and take liberties with his everlasting laws of right and wrong; and so fancy, that provided we talk of the meek and lowly Jesus, and of his blood washing away all our sins, that we are free to behave very much as if Jesus had never come into the world to teach men their duty, and free to commit almost any sin which does not disgrace us among our neighbours, or render us punishable by the law.

My friends, it is *not so.* And those who fancy that it is so, will find out their mistake bitterly enough. Infinite love and forgiveness to those who repent and amend and do right; but infinite rigour and punishment to those who will not amend and do right. This is the everlasting law of God's universe; and every soul of man will find it out at last, and find that the Lord Jesus Christ is not a Being to be trifled with, and that the precious blood which he shed on the cross is of no avail to those who are not minded to be righteous even as he is righteous.

'But Christ is so loving, so tender-hearted that he surely will not punish us for our sins.' This is the confused notion that too many people have about him. And the answer to it is, that just *because* Christ is so loving, so tender-hearted, there-fore he *must* punish us for our sins, unless we utterly give up our sins, and do right instead of wrong.

That false notion springs out of men's selfishness. They think of sin as something which only hurts themselves; when they do wrong they think merely, 'What punishment will God inflict on *me* for doing wrong?' They are wrapt up in themselves. They forget that their sins are not merely a matter between them and Christ, but between them and their neighbours; that every wrong action they commit, every wrong word they speak, every wrong habit in which they indulge themselves, sooner or later, more or less hurts their neighbours—ay, hurts all mankind.

And does Christ care only for *them?* Does he not care for their neighbours? Has he not all mankind to provide for, and govern and guide? And can he allow bad men to go on making this world worse, without punishing them, any more than a gardener can allow weeds to hurt his flowers, and not root them up? What would you say of a man who was so merciful to the weeds that he let them choke the flowers? What would you say of a shepherd who was so merciful to the wolves that he let them eat his sheep? What would you say of a magistrate who was so merciful to thieves that he let them rob the honest men ? And do you fancy that Christ is a less careful and just governor of the world than the magistrate who punishes the thief that honest men may live in safety ?

Not so.   Not only will Christ punish the wolves who devour his sheep, but he will punish his sheep themselves if they hurt each other, torment each other, lead each other astray, or in any way inter- fere with the just and equal rule of his kingdom ; and this, not out of spite or cruelty, but simply because he is perfect love.

Go, therefore, and think of Christ this Passion Week as he was, and is, and ever will be.   Think of the whole Christ, and not of some part of his character which may specially please your fancy. Think of him as the patient and forgiving Christ, who prayed for his murderers, 'Father, forgive them, for they know not what they do.'   But remember that, in this very Passion Week, there came out of those most gentle lips—the lips which blessed little children, and cried to all who were weary and heavy laden, to come to him and he would give them rest—that out of those most gentle lips, I say, in this very Passion Week, there went forth the most awful threats which ever were uttered, 'Woe unto you, Scribes and Pharisees, hypocrites. Ye serpents, ye generation of vipers, how can ye escape the damnation of hell?' Think of him as the Lamb who offered himself freely on the cross for sinners. But think of him, too, as the Lamb who shall one day come in glory to judge all men according to their works, Think of him as full of boundless tenderness and humanity, boundless long-suffering and mercy. But remember that beneath that boundless sweetness and tenderness there burns a consuming fire; a fire of divine scorn and indignation against all who sin, like Pharaoh, out of cruelty and pride; against all which is foul and brutal, mean and base, false and hypocritical, cruel and unjust; a fire which burns, and will burn against all the wickedness which is done on earth, and all the misery and sorrow which is suffered on earth, till the Lord has burned it up for ever, and there is nothing but love and justice, order and usefulness, peace and happiness, left in the universe of God.

Oh, think of these things, and cast away your sins betimes, at the foot of his everlasting cross, lest you be consumed with your sins in his everlasting fire!

SERMON XII.

THE BIRTHNIGHT OF FREEDOM.

(Easter Day.)

EXODUS xii. 42.

This is a night to be much observed unto the Lord, for bringing the children of Israel out of Egypt.

TO be much observed unto the Lord by the children of Israel. And by us, too, my friends; and by all nations who call themselves *free*.

There are many and good ways of looking at Easter Day. Let us look at it in this way for once.

It is the day on which God himself set men *free*.

Consider the story. These Isràelites, the children of Abraham, the brave, wild patriarch of the desert, have been settled for hundreds of years in the rich lowlands of Egypt. There they have been eating and drinking their fill, and grow-ing more weak, slavish, luxurious, fonder and fonder of the flesh-pots of Egypt; fattening liter-ally for the slaughter, like beasts in a stall. They are spiritually dead—dead in trespasses and sins. They do not want to be free, to be a nation. They are content to be slaves and idolaters, if they can only fill their stomachs. This is the spiritual death of a nation.

I say, they do not want to be free. When they are oppressed, they cry out—as an animal cries when you beat him. But after they are free, when they get into danger, or miss their meat, they cry out too, and are willing enough to return to slavery; as the dog which has run away for fear of the whip, will go back to his kennel for the sake of his food. 'Because there were no graves in Egypt, hast thou taken us away to die in the wilderness? Wherefore hast thou dealt thus with us to carry us out of Egypt?' And again, 'Would God we had died by the hand of the Lord in the land of Egypt, where we did sit by the flesh-pots, and eat meat to the full!' *Brutalized*, in one word, were these poor children of Israel.

Then God took their cause into his own hand;

I say emphatically into his own hand. If that part of the story be not true, I care nothing for the rest. If God did not personally and actually interfere on behalf of those poor slaves; if the plagues of Egypt are not *true*—if the passage of the Red Sea be not *true*—the story tells me and you nothing; gives us no hope for ourselves, no hope for mankind.

For see. One says, and truly, God is good; God is love; God is just; God hates oppression and wrong.

But if God be love, he must surely show his love by doing loving things.

If God be just, he must show his justice by doing just things.

If God hates oppression, then he must free the oppressed.

If God hates wrong, then he must set the wrong right.

For what would you think of a man who professed to be loving and just, and to hate oppression and wrong, and yet never took the trouble to do a good action, or to put down wrong, when he had the power? You would call him a hypocrite; you would think his love and justice very much on his tongue, and not in his heart.

And will you believe that God is like that man? God forbid!

Comfortable scholars and luxurious ladies may content themselves with a *dead* God, who does not interfere to help the oppressed, to right the wrong, to bind up the broken-hearted; but men and women who work, who sorrow, who suffer, who partake of all the ills which flesh is heir to—they want a *living* God, an acting God, a God who *will* interfere to right the wrong. Yes—they want a living God. And they have a living God—even the God who interfered to bring the Israelites out of Egypt with signs and wonders, and a mighty hand and an outstretched arm, and executed judgment upon Pharaoh and his proud and cruel hosts. And when they read in the Bible of that God, when they read in their Bibles the story of the Exodus, their hearts answer, *This* is right. This is the God whom we need. This is what ought to have happened. This is true: for it must be true. Let comfortable folks who know no sorrow trouble their brains as to whether sixty or six hundred thousand fighting men came out of Egypt with Moses. We care not for numbers. What we care for is, not how many came out, but who brought them out, and that he who brought

them out was *God*.   And the book which tells us
that, we will cling to, will love, will reverence above
all the books on earth, because it tells of a living
God, who works and acts and interferes for men;
who not only hates wrong, but rights wrong; not
only hates oppression, but puts oppressors down;
not only pities the oppressed, but sets the
oppressed free; a God who not only wills that
man should have freedom, but sent freedom down
to him from heaven.

Scholars have said that the old Greeks were the
fathers of freedom; and there have been other
peoples in the world's history who have made
glorious and successful struggles to throw off their
tyrants and be free.   And they have said, We are
the fathers of freedom; liberty was born with us.
Not so, my friends!   Liberty is of a far older and
far nobler house; Liberty was born, if you will
receive it, on the first Easter night, on the night
to be much remembered among the children of
Israel—ay, among all mankind—when God himself stooped from heaven to set the oppressed free.
Then was freedom born.   Not in the counsels of
men, however wise; or in the battles of men,
however brave: but in the counsels of God, and
the battle of God—amid human agony and terror,

and the shaking of the heaven and the earth; amid the great cry throughout Egypt when a first-born son lay dead in every house; and the tempest which swept aside the Red Sea waves; and the pillar of cloud by day, and the pillar of fire by night; and the Red Sea shore covered with the corpses of the Egyptians; and the thunderings and lightnings and earthquakes of Sinai; and the sound as of a trumpet waxing loud and long; and the voice, most human and most divine, which spake from off the lonely mountain peak to that vast horde of coward and degenerate slaves, and said, 'I am the Lord thy God who brought thee out of the land of Egypt. Thou shalt obey my laws, and keep my commandments to do them.' Oh! the man who would rob his suffering fellow-creatures of that story—he knows not how deep and bitter are the needs of man.

Then was freedom born: but not of man; not of the will of the flesh, nor of the will of man, but of the will of God, from whom all good things come; and of Christ, who is the life and the light of men and of nations, and of the whole world, and of all worlds, past, present, and to come.

From God came freedom. To be used as his gift, according to his laws; for he gave, and he can take away; as it is written, 'He shall take the kingdom of God from you, and give it to a people bringing forth the fruits thereof.' 'For there be many first that shall be last; and last that shall be first.' It is this which makes the Jews indeed a peculiar people : the thought that the living God had actually and really done for them what they could not do for themselves; that he had made them a nation, and not they themselves. It is this which makes the Old Testament an utterly different book, with an utterly different lesson, to the written history of any other nation in the world.

And yet it is this which makes the history of the Jews the key to every other history in the world. For in it Jesus Christ our Lord, the living God who makes history, who governs all nations, reveals and unveils himself, and teaches not the Jews only, but us and all nations, that it is he who hath made us, and not we ourselves; that we got not the land in possession by our own sword, nor was it our own strength that helped us, but thou, O Lord, because thou hadst a favour unto us; that not to us, not to us is the praise of any national greatness or glory, but to God, from whom it comes as surely a free gift as the gift of liberty to the Jews of old.

I say, the history of the Jews is the history of the whole Church, and of every nation in Christendom.

As with the Jews, so with the nations of Europe; whenever they have trusted in themselves, their own power and wisdom, they have ended in weakness and folly. Whenever they have trusted in Christ the living God, and said, 'It is he that hath made us, and not we ourselves,' they have risen to strength and wisdom. When they have forgotten the living God, national life and patriotism have died in them, as they died in the Jews. When they have remembered that the most high God was their Redeemer, then in them, as in the Jews, have national life and patriotism revived.

And as it was with the Jews in the wilderness, so it has been with them since Christ's resurrection. They fancied that they were going at once into the promised land. So did the first Christians. But the Jews had to wander forty years in the wilderness; and Christendom has had to wander too, in strange and bloodstained paths, for one thousand eight hundred years and more. For why? The Israelites were not worthy to enter at once into rest; no more have the nation of Christ's Church been worthy. The Israelites brought out of Egypt base and slavish passions, which had to be purged out of them ; so have we out of heathendom. They brought out, too, heathen superstitions, and mixed them up with the worship of God, bearing about in the wilderness the tabernacle of Moloch and the image of their god Remphan, and making the calf in Horeb; and so, alas! again and again, has the Church of Christ.

Nay, the whole generation, save two, who came out of Egypt, had to die in the wilderness, and leave their bones scattered far and wide. And so has mankind been dying, by war and by disease, and by many fearful scourges besides what is called now-a-days, natural decay.

But all the while a new generation was springing up, trained in the wilderness to be bold and hardy ; trained, too, under Moses' stern law, to the fear of God ; to reverence, and discipline, and obedience, without which freedom is merely brutal license, and a nation is no nation, but a mere flock of sheep or a herd of wolves.

And so, for these one thousand eight hundred years have the generations of Christendom, by the training of the Church and the light of the Gospel, been growing in wisdom and knowledge ;

growing in morality and humanity, in that true discipline and loyalty which are the yoke-fellows of freedom and independence, to make them fit for that higher state, that heavenly Canaan, of which we know not *when* it will come, nor whether its place will be on this earth or else-where ; but of which it is written, 'And I John saw the holy city, New Jerusalem, coming down from God out of heaven, prepared as a bride adorned for her husband. And I heard a great voice out of heaven saying, Behold, the taber-nacle of God is with men, and he will dwell with them, and they shall be his people, and God himself shall be with them, and be their God. And God shall wipe away all tears from their eyes; and there shall be no more death, neither sorrow, nor crying, neither shall there be any more pain: for the former things are passed away. And he that sat upon the throne said, Behold, I make all things new.

'And I saw no temple therein : for the Lord God Almighty and the Lamb are the temple of it. And the city had no need of the sun, neither of the moon to shine in it: for the glory of God did lighten it, and the Lamb is the light thereof. And the nations of them which are saved shall walk in the light of it ; and the kings of the earth do bring their glory and honour into it. And the gates of it shall not be shut at all by day : for there shall be no night there. And they shall bring the glory and honour of the nations into it. And there shall in no wise enter into it anything that defileth, neither whatsoever worketh abomination or maketh a lie : but they which are written in the Lamb's book of life.'

That, the perfect Easter Day, seems far enough off as yet ; but it will come. As the Lord liveth, it will come; and to it may Christ in his mercy bring us all, and our children's children after us. Amen.

SERMON XIII.

KORAH, DATHAN, AND ABIRAM.

(First Sunday after Easter, 1863.)

NUMBERS xvi. 32—35.

And the earth opened her mouth, and swallowed them up, and their houses, and all the men that appertained unto Korah, and all their goods. They, and all that appertained to them, went down alive into the pit, and the earth closed upon them: and they perished from among the congregation. And all Israel that were round about them fled at the cry of them: for they said, Lest the earth swallow us up also. And there came out a fire from the Lord, and consumed the two hundred and fifty men that offered incense.

I WILL begin by saying that there are several things in this chapter which I do not understand, and cannot explain to you. Be it so. That is no reason why we should not look at the parts of the chapter which we can understand and can explain.

There are matters without end in the world round us, and in our own hearts, and in the life of every one, which we cannot explain; and therefore we need not be surprised to find things which we cannot explain in the life and history of the most remarkable nation upon earth—the nation whose business it has been to teach all other nations the knowledge of the true God, and who was specially and curiously trained for that work.

But the one broad common-sense lesson of this chapter, it seems to me, is one which is on the very surface of it; one which every true Englishman at least will see, and see to be true, when he hears the chapter read; and that is, the necessity of *discipline*.

God has brought the Israelites out of Egypt, and set them free. One of the first lessons which they have to learn is, that freedom does not mean license and discord—does not mean every one doing that which is right in the sight of his own eyes. From that springs self-will, division, quarrels, revolt, civil war, weakness, profligacy, and ruin to the whole people. Without order, discipline, obedience to law, there can be no true and lasting freedom; and, therefore, order must be kept at all risks, the law obeyed, and rebellion punished.

Now rebellion may be and ought to be punished

far more severely in some cases than in others. If men rebel here, in Great Britain or Ireland, we smile at them, and let them off with a slight imprisonment, because we are not afraid of them. They can do no harm.

But there are cases in which rebellion must be punished with a swift and sharp hand. On board a ship at sea, for instance, where the safety of the whole ship, the lives of the whole crew, depend on instant obedience, mutiny may be punished by death on the spot. Many a commander has ere now, and rightly too, struck down the rebel without trial or argument; and ended him and his mutiny on the spot; by the sound rule that it is expedient that one man die for the people, and that the whole nation perish not.

And so it was with the Israelites in the desert. All depended on their obedience. God had given them a law—a constitution, as we should say now—perfectly fitted, no doubt, for them. If they once began to rebel and mutiny against that law, all was over with them. That great, foolish, ignorant multitude would have broken up, probably fought among themselves—certainly parted company, and either starved in the desert, or have been destroyed piecemeal by the wild warlike tribes, Midianites, Moabites, Amalekites — who were ready enough for slaughter and plunder. They would never have reached Canaan. They would never have become a great nation. So they had to be, by necessity, under martial law. The word must be, Obey or die. As for any cruelty in putting Korah, Dathan, and Abiram to death, it was worth the death of a hundred such—or a thousand—to preserve the great and glorious nation of the Jews to be the teachers of the world.

Now this Korah, Dathan, and Abiram rebel. They rebel against Moses about a question of the priesthood. It really matters little to us what that question was—it was a question of Moses' law, which, of course, is now done away. Only remember this, that these men were princes— great feudal noblemen, as we should say; and that they rebelled on the strength of their rank and their rights as noblemen to make laws for them- selves and for the people; and that the mob of their dependents seem to have been inclined to support them.

Surely if Moses had executed martial law on them with his own hand, he would have been as perfectly justified as a captain of a ship of war or a general of an army would be now.

But he did not do so. And why? Because *Moses* did not bring the people out of Egypt. Moses was not their king. *God* brought them out of Egypt. God was their king. That was the lesson which they had to learn, and to teach other nations also. They have rebelled, not against Moses, but against God ; and not Moses, but God must punish, and show that he is not a dead God, but a living God, one who can defend himself, and enforce his own laws, and execute judgment—and, if need be, vengeance—without needing any man to fight his battles for him.

And God does so. The powers of Nature—the earthquake and the nether fire—shall punish these rebels ; and so they do.

'And Moses said, Hereby ye shall know that the Lord hath sent me to do all these works ; for I have not done them of mine own mind. If these men die the common death of all men, or if they be visited after the visitation of all men ; then the Lord hath not sent me. But if the Lord make a new thing, and the earth open her mouth and swallow them up, with all that appertain to them, and they go down quick into the pit ; then ye shall understand that these men have provoked the Lord.'

Men have thought differently of the story; but I call it a righteous story, and a noble story, and one which agrees with my conscience, and my reason, and my notion of what ought to be, and my experience also of what is—of the way in which God's world is governed unto this day.

What then are we to think of the earth opening and swallowing them up? What are we to think of a fire coming out from the Lord, and consuming two hundred and fifty men that offered incense?

This first. That discipline and order are so absolutely necessary for the well-being of a nation that they must be kept at all risks, and enforced by the most terrible punishments.

It seems to me (to speak with all reverence) as if God had said to the Jews, 'I have set you free. I will make of you a great nation; I will lead you into a good land and large. But if you are to be a great nation, if you are to conquer that good land and large, you must obey: and you shall obey. The earthquake and the fire shall teach you to obey, and make you an example to the rest of the Israelites, and to all nations after you.'

But how hard, some may think, that the wives and the children should suffer for their parents' sins.

My friends, we do not know that a single woman or child died then for whom it was not better that he or she should die. That is one of the deep things which we must leave to the perfect justice and mercy of God.

And next—what is it after all, but what we see going on round us all the day long? God does visit the sins of the fathers on the children. There is no denying it. Wives do suffer for their husbands' sins; children and children's children for whole generations after generations suffer for their parents' sins, and become unhealthy, or superstitious, or profligate, or poor, or slavish, because their parents sinned, and dragged down their children with them in their fall. It is a law of the world; and therefore it is a law of God. And it is reasonable to be believed that God might choose to teach the Israelites, once and for all, that it *was* a law of his world. For by swallowing up those women and children with the men, God said to the Israelites, it seems to me in a way which could not be mistaken, ' This is the consequence of lawlessness and disorder—that you not only injure yourselves, but your children after you, and involve your families in the same ruin as yourselves.'

But there was another lesson, and a deep lesson,

in the earthquake and in the fire. And what was
this? that the earthquake and the fire came out
from the Lord.

Earthquakes have swallowed up not hundreds
merely, but many thousands, in many countries,
and at many times.

Fire has come forth, and still comes forth from
the ground, from the clouds, from the consequences
of man's own carelessness, and destroys beast and
man, and the works of man's hands. Then men
ask in terror and doubt, 'Who sends the earthquake and the fire? Do they come from the
devil—the destroyer? Do they come by chance,
from some brute and blind powers of nature?'

This chapter answers, 'No. They come from
the Lord, from whom all good things do come ;
from the Lord who delivered the Israelites out of
Egypt ; who so loved the world that he spared
not his only begotten Son, but freely gave him
for us.'

Now I say that is a gospel, and good news,
which we want now as much as ever men did ;
which the children of Israel wanted then, though
not one whit more than we.

Many hundreds of years had these Israelites
been in Egypt. Storm, lightning, earthquake, the

fires of the burning mountains, were things unknown to them. They were going into Canaan—
a good land and fruitful, but a land of storms and
thunders ; a land, too, of earthquakes and subter-
ranean fires. The deepest earthquake-crack in the
world is the valley of the Jordan, ending in the
Dead Sea—a long valley, through which at different points the nether fires of the earth even now
burst up at times. In Abraham's time they had
destroyed the five cities of the plain. The prophets mention them, especially Isaiah and Micah,
as breaking out again in their own times ; and in
our own lifetime earthquake and fire have done
fearful destruction in the north part of the Holy
Land.

Now what was to prevent the Israelites worshipping the earthquake and the fire as gods ?

Nothing. Conceive the terror and horror of the
Jews coming out of that quiet land of Egypt,
the first time they felt the ground rocking and
rolling ; the first time they heard the roar of the
earthquake beneath their feet ; the first time they
saw, in the magnificent words of Micah, the mountains molten and the valleys cleft as wax before
the fire, like water poured down a steep place ;
and discovered that beneath their very feet was

Tophet, the pit of fire and brimstone, ready to burst up and overwhelm them they knew not when.

What could they do, but what the Canaanites did who dwelt already in that land ? What but to say, 'The fire is king. The fire is the great and dreadful God, and to him we must pray, lest he devour us up.' For so did the Canaanites. They called the fire Moloch, which means simply the king ; and they worshipped this fire-king, and made idols of him, and offered human sacrifices to him. They had idols of metal, before which an everlasting fire burned ; and on the arms of the idol the priests laid the children who were to be sacrificed, that they might roll down into the fire and be burnt alive. That is actual fact. In one case, which we know of well, hundreds of years after Moses' time, the Carthaginians offered two hundred boys of their best families to Moloch in one day. This is that making the children pass through the fire to Moloch—burning them in the fire to Moloch—of which we read several times in the Old Testament ; as ugly and accursed a superstition as men ever invented.

What deliverance was there for them from these abominable superstitions, except to know that the fire-kingdom was God's kingdom, and not Moloch's at all; to know with Micah and with David that the hills were molten like wax *before the presence of the Lord;* that it was the blast of his breath which discovered the foundations of the world ; that it was *he* who made the sea flee and drove back the Jordan stream ; that it was before *him* that the mountains skipped like rams and the little hills like young sheep ; that the battles of shaking were God's battles, with which he could fight for his people ; that it was he who ordained Tophet, and whose spirit kindled it.   That it was he—and that too in mercy as well as anger—who visited the land in Isaiah's time with thunder and earthquake, and great noise, and storm and tempest, and the flame of devouring fire.   That the earth opened and swallowed up those whom God chose, and no others.   That if fire came forth, it came forth from the Lord, and burned where and what God chose, and nothing else.   Yes.   If you will only understand, once and for all, that the history of the Jews is the history of the Lord's turning a people from the cowardly, slavish worship of sun and stars, of earthquakes and burning mountains, and all the brute powers of nature which the heathen worshipped, and teaching them to trust and obey him,

the living God, the Lord and Master of all, then
the Old Testament will be clear to you throughout ; but if not, then not.

You cannot read your Bibles without seeing
how that great lesson was stamped into the very
hearts of the Hebrew prophets; how they are
continually speaking of the fire and the earthquake, and yet continually declaring that they too
obey God and do God's will, and that the man
who fears God need not fear them—that God was
their hope and strength, a very present help in
trouble. Therefore would they not fear, though
the earth was moved, and though the mountains
be carried into the midst of the sea.

And we, too, need the same lesson in these
scientific days. We too need to fix it in our
hearts, that the powers of nature are the powers
of God; that he orders them by his providence to
do what he will, and when and where he will ;
that, as the Psalmist says, the winds are his mes-
sengers and the flames of fire his ministers. And
this we shall learn from the Bible, and from no
other book whatsoever.

God taught the Jews this, by a strange and
miraculous education, that they might teach it in
their turn to all mankind. And they have taught

it. For the Bible bids us—as no other book does—not to be afraid of the world on which we live; not to be afraid of earthquake or tempest, or any of the powers of nature which seem to us terrible and cruel, and destroying; for they are the powers of the good and just and loving God. They obey our Father in heaven, without whom not a sparrow falls to the ground, and our Lord Jesus Christ, who came not to destroy men's lives, but to save them. And therefore we need not fear them, or look on them with any blind superstition, as things too awful for us to search into. We may search into their causes; find out, if we can, the laws which they obey, because those laws are given them by God our Father; try, by using those laws, to escape them, as we are learning now to escape tempests; or to prevent them, as we are learning now to prevent pestilences: and where we cannot do that, face them manfully, saying, 'It is my Father's will. These terrible events must be doing God's work. They may be punishing the guilty; they may be taking the righteous away from the evil to come; they may be teaching wise men lessons which will enable them years hence to save lives without number; they may be preparing the face of the earth for the use of generations yet unborn.   Whatever they are doing they are and must be doing good; for they are doing the will of the living Father, who willeth that none should perish, and hateth nothing that he hath made.'

This, my friends, is the lesson which the Bible teaches; and because it teaches that lesson it is the Book of books, and the inspired word or message, not of men concerning God, but of God himself, concerning himself, his kingdom over this world and over all worlds, and his good will to men.

SERMON XIV.

BALAAM.

NUMBERS xxiii. 19.

God is not a man, that he should lie; neither the son of man, that
he should repent: hath he said, and shall he not do it? or hath
he spoken, and shall he not make it good?

IF I was asked for any proof that the story of
Balaam, as I find it in the Bible, is a true
story, I should lay my hand on this one only—
and that is, the deep knowledge of human nature
which is shown in it.

The character of Balaam is so perfectly natural,
and yet of a kind so very difficult to unravel
and explain, that if the story was invented by
man, as poems or novels are, it must have
been invented very late indeed in the history
of the Jews; at a time when they had grown
to be a far more civilised people, far more experienced in the cunning tricks of the human
heart than they were, as far as we can see

from the Bible, before the Babylonish captivity. But it was *not* invented late; for no Jew in these later times would have thought of making Balaam, a heathen, to be a prophet of God, or a believer in the true God at all. The later Jews took up the notion that God spoke to and cared for the Jews only, and that all other nations were accursed.

There is no reason, therefore, against simply believing the story as it stands. It seems a very ancient story indeed, suiting exactly in its smallest details the place where Moses, or whoever wrote the Book of Numbers, has put it.

We, in these days, are accustomed to draw a sharp line between the good and the bad, the converted and the unconverted, the children of God and the children of this world, those who have God's Spirit and those who have not, which we find nowhere in Scripture; and therefore when we read of such a man as Balaam we cannot understand him. He is a bad man, but yet he is a prophet. How can that be? He knows the true God. More, he has the Spirit of God in him, and thereby utters deep and wonderful prophecies; and yet he is a bad man and a rogue. How can that be?

The puzzle, my friends, is one of our own

making. If, instead of taking up doctrines out of books, we will use our own eyes and ears and common sense, and look honestly at this world as it is, and men and women as they are, we shall find nothing unnatural or strange in Balaam ; we shall find him very like a good many people whom we know ; very like—nay, probably, too like— ourselves in some particulars.

Now bear in mind, first, that Balaam is no impostor or magician. He is a wise man, and a prophet of God. God really speaks to him, and really inspires him.

And bear in mind, too, that Balaam's inspiration did not merely open his mouth to say wonderful words which he did not understand, but opened his heart to say righteous and wise things which he did understand.

'Remember,' says the prophet Micah, 'O my people, what Balak, king of Moab, consulted, and what Balaam, the son of Beor, answered him from Shittim unto Gilgal, that ye may know the right- eousness of the Lord. Wherewith shall I come before the Lord, and bow myself before the high God ? Shall I come before him with burnt offer- ings, with calves of a year old ? Will the Lord be pleased with thousands of rams, or with ten thousands of rivers of oil? Shall I give my first-born for my transgressions, the fruit of my body for the sin of my soul? He hath shewed thee, O man, what is good, and what doth the Lord require of . thee, but to do justly, and to love mercy, and to walk humbly with thy God.' Why, what deeper or wiser words are there in the whole Old Testament? This man Balaam had seen down into the deepest depths of all morality, unto the deepest depths of all religion. The man who knew that, knew more than ninety-nine in a hundred do even in a Christian country now, and more than nine hundred and ninety-nine thousand nine hundred and ninety-nine in a million knew in those days. Let no one, after that speech, doubt that Balaam was indeed a prophet of the Lord; and yet he was a bad man, and came deservedly to a bad end.

So much easier, my friends, is it to know what is right than to do what is right.

What then was wrong in Balaam?

This, that he was double-minded. He wished to serve God. True. But he wished to serve himself by serving God, as too many do in all times.

That was what was wrong with him—self-seeking; and the Bible story brings out that self-seeking with a delicacy, a keenness, and a perfect knowledge of human nature, which ought to teach us some of the secrets of our own hearts.

Watch how Balaam, as a matter of course, inquires of the Lord whether he may go, and refuses, seemingly at first honestly.

Then how the temptation grows on him; how, when he feels tempted, he fights against it in fine-sounding professions, just because he feels that he is going to yield to it. Then how he begins to tempt God, by asking him again, in hopes that God may have changed his mind. Then when he has his foolish wish granted he goes. Then when the terrible warning comes to him that he is on the wrong road, that God's wrath is gone out against him, and his angel ready to destroy him, he is full still of hollow professions of obedience, instead of casting himself utterly upon God's mercy, and confessing his sin, and entreating pardon.

Then how, instead of being frightened at God's letting him have his way, he is emboldened by it to tempt God more and more, and begins offering bullocks and rams on altars, first in this place and then in that, in hopes still that God may change his mind, and let him curse Israel; in hopes that God may be like one of the idols of the heathen, who could (so the heathen thought) be coaxed and flattered round by sacrifices to do whatever their worshippers wished.

Then, when he finds that all is of no use; that he must not curse Israel, and must not earn Balak's silver and gold, he is forced to be an honest man in spite of himself; and therefore he makes the best of his disappointment by taking mighty credit to himself for being honest, while he wishes all the while he might have been allowed to have been dishonest. Oh, if all this is not poor human nature, drawn by the pen of a truly inspired writer, what is it?

Moreover, it is curious to watch how as Balaam is forced step by step to be an honest man, so step by step he rises. A weight falls off his mind and heart, and the Spirit of God comes upon him.

He feels for once that he must speak his mind, that he must obey God. As he looks down from off the mountain top, and sees the vast encampment of the Israelites spread over the vale below, for miles and miles, as far as the eye can see, all ordered, disciplined, arranged according to their tribes, the Spirit of God comes upon him, and he gives way to it and speaks.

The sight of that magnificent array wakens up in him the thought of how divine is order, how strong is order, how order is the life and root of a nation, and how much more, when that order is the order of God.

'How goodly are thy tents, O Jacob, and thy tabernacles, O Israel! As the valleys are they spread forth, as gardens by the river's side, as the trees of lign aloes which the Lord hath planted, and as cedar trees beside the waters. His king shall be higher than Agag,' and all his wild Amalekite hordes. He will be a true nation, civilized, ordered, loyal and united, for God is teaching him.

Who can resist such a nation as that? 'God has brought him out of Egypt. He has the strength of an unicorn.' 'I shall see him,' he says, 'but not now; I shall behold him, but not nigh: there shall come a Star out of Jacob, and a Sceptre shall rise out of Israel, and shall smite the corners of Moab, and destroy all the children of Sheth.' And when he looked on Amalek, he took up his parable, and said, 'Amalek was the first of the nation; but his latter end shall be that he perish for ever.' And he looked on the Kenites, and took up his parable, and said, 'Strong is thy dwelling-place, and thou puttest thy nest in a rock. Nevertheless, the Kenite shall be wasted, till Asshur shall carry thee away captive.' 'Alas, who shall live when God doeth this !'

And then, beyond all, after all the Canaanites and other Syrian races have been destroyed, he sees, dimly and afar off, another destruction still.

In his home in the far east the fame of the ships of Chittim has reached him ; the fame of the new people, the sea-roving heroes of the Greeks, of whom old Homer sang; the handsomest, cunningest, most daring of mankind, who are spreading their little trading colonies along all the isles and shores, as we now are spreading ours over the world. Those ships of Chittim, too, have a great and glorious future before them. Some day or other they will come and afflict Asshur, the great empire of the East, out of which Balaam probably came; and afflict Eber too, the kingdom of the Jews, and they too shall perish for ever.

Dimly he sees it, for it is very far away. But that it will come he sees; and beyond that all is dark. He has said his say; he has spoken the whole truth for once.   Balak's house full of silver and gold would not have bought him off and stopped his mouth when such awful thoughts crowded on his mind.   So he returns to his place—to do what?

If he cannot earn Balak's gold by cursing Israel, he can do it by giving him cunning and politic advice.   He advises Balak to make friends with the Israelites and mix them up with his people by enticing them to the feasts of his idols, at which the women threw themselves away in shameful profligacy, after the custom of the heathens of these parts.

In the next chapter we read how Moses, and Phinehas, Aaron's grandson, put down those filthy abominations with a high hand ; and how Balaam's detestable plot, instead of making peace, makes war ; and in chapter xxxi. you read the terrible destruction of the whole nation of the Midianites, and among it this one short and terrible hint : 'Balaam also, the son of Beor, they slew with the sword.'

But what may we learn from this ugly story ?

Recollect what I said at first, that we should find Balaam too like many people now-a-days ; perhaps too like ourselves.

Too like indeed. For never were men more tempted to sin as Balaam did than in these days, when religion is all the fashion, and pays a man, and helps him on in life; when, indeed, a man cannot expect to succeed without professing some sort of religion or other.

Thereby comes a terrible temptation to many men. I do not mean to hypocrites, but to really well-meaning men. They like religion. They wish to be good; they have the feeling of devotion. They pray, they read their Bibles, they are attentive to services and to sermons, and are more or less pious people. But soon—too soon—they find that their piety is profitable. Their business increases. Their credit increases. They are trusted and respected; their advice is asked and taken. They gain power over their fellow-men. What a fine thing it is, they think, to bé pious!

Then creeps in the love of the world; the love of money, or power, or admiration; and they begin to value religion because it helps them to get on in the world. They begin more and more to love piety not for its own sake, but for the sake of what it brings; not because it pleases God, but because it pleases the world; not because it enables them to help their fellow-men, but because it enables them to help themselves.

So they get double-minded, unstable, inconsistent, as St. James says, in all their ways; trying to serve God and Mammon at once. Trying to do good—as long as doing good does not hurt them in the world's eyes; but longing oftener and oftener to do wrong, if only God would not be angry. Then comes on Balaam's frame of mind, 'If Balak would give me his house full of silver and gold, I cannot go beyond the commandment of the Lord.'

Oh no. They would not do a wrong thing for the world—only they must be quite sure first that it is wrong. Has God really forbidden it? Why should they not take care of their interest? Why should they not get on in the world? So they begin, like Balaam, to tempt God, to see how far they can go; to see if God has forbidden this and that mean, or cowardly, or covetous, or ambitious deed. So they soon settle for themselves what God has forbidden and what he has not; and their rule of life becomes this—that whatsoever is safe and whatsoever is profitable is pretty sure to be right; and after that no wonder if, like Balaam, they indulge themselves in every sort of sin, provided only it is respectable, and does not hurt them in the world's eyes.

And all the while they keep up their religion. Ay, they are often more attentive than ever to religion, because their consciences pinch them at times, and have to be silenced and drugged by continual church-goings and chapel-goings, and readings and prayings, in order that they may be able to say to themselves with Balaam, 'Thus saith Balaam, he who heard the word of God, and had the knowledge of the Most High.'

So they say to themselves, 'I must be right. How religious I am ; how fond of sermons, and of church services, and church restorations, and missionary meetings, and charitable institutions, and everything that is good and pious. I *must* be right with God.' Deceiving their ownselves, and saying to themselves, 'I am rich and increased with goods, I have need of nothing,' and not knowing that they are wretched, and miserable, and blind, and naked.

Would God that such people, of whom there are too many, would take St. John's warning and buy of the Lord gold tried in the fire—the true gold of honesty—that they may be truly rich, and anoint their eyes with eye-salve that they may see themselves for once as they are.

But what does this story teach us concerning God? For remember, as I tell you every Sunday, that each fresh story in the Pentateuch reveals to us something fresh about the character of God. What does Balaam's story reveal? Balaam himself tells us in the text, 'God is not a man that he should lie, nor the son of man that he should repent. Hath he said, and shall he not do it?'

Yes. Fancy not that any wishes or prayers of yours can persuade God to alter his everlasting laws of right and wrong. If he has commanded a thing, he has commanded it because it is according to his everlasting laws, which cannot change, because they are made in his eternal image and likeness. Therefore if God has commanded you a thing, *do it* heartily, fully, without arguing or complaining. If you begin arguing with God's law, excusing yourself from it, inventing reasons why *you* need not obey it in this particular instance, though every one else ought, then you will end, like Balaam, in disobeying the law, and it will grind you to powder.

But if you obey God's law honestly, with a single eye and a whole heart, you will find in it a blessing, and peace, and strength, and everlasting life.

SERMON XV.

DEUTERONOMY.

(Third Sunday after Easter.)

DEUT. iv. 39, 40.

Know therefore this day, and consider it in thine heart, that
the Lord he is God in heaven above, and upon the earth beneath: there is none else.   Thou shalt keep therefore his statutes
and his commandments, which I command thee this day, that
it may go well with thee, and with thy children after thee,
and that thou mayest prolong thy days upon the earth, which
the Lord thy God giveth thee, for ever.

LEARNED men have argued much of late
as to who wrote the book of Deuteronomy.
After having read a good deal on the subject,
I can only say that I see no reason why we
should not believe the ancient account which
the Jews give, that it was written, or at least
spoken by Moses.

No doubt there are difficulties in the book.
If there had not been, there would never have

been any dispute about the matter; but the plain, broad, common-sense case is this:

The book of Deuteronomy is made up of several great orations or sermons, delivered, says the work itself, by Moses, to the whole people of the Jews, before they left the wilderness and entered into the land of Canaan ; wherefore it is called Deuteronomy, or the second law. In it some small matters of the law are altered, as was to be expected, when the Jews were going to change their place and their whole way of life. But the whole teaching and meaning of the book is exactly that of Exodus and Leviticus. Moreover, it is, if possible, the grandest and deepest book of the Old Testament. Its depth and wisdom are unequalled. I hold it to be the sum and substance of all political philosophy and morality of the true life of a nation. The books of Isaiah, Jeremiah, and Ezekiel, grand as they are, are, as it were, its children ; growths out of the root which Deuteronomy reveals.

Now if Moses did not write it, who did?

As for the style of it being different from that of Exodus and Leviticus, the simple answer is, Why not? They are books of history and of laws. This is a book of sermons or orations, spoken first, and not written, which, of course, would be in a different style. Besides, why should not Moses have spoken differently at the end of forty years' such experience as never man had before or since? Every one who thinks, writes, or speaks in public, knows how his style alters, as fresh knowledge and experience come to him. Are you to suppose that Moses gained nothing by *his* experience?

As for a few texts in it being like Isaiah or Jeremiah, they are likely enough to be so; for if (as I believe) Deuteronomy was written long before those books, what more likely than that Isaiah and Jeremiah should have studied it, and taken some of its words to themselves when they were preaching to the Jews just what Deuteronomy preaches?

As for any one else having written it in Moses' name, hundreds of years after his death, I cannot believe it. If there had been in Israel a prophet great and wise enough to write Deuteronomy, we must have heard more about him, for he must have been famous at the time when he did live; while, if he were great enough to write Deuteronomy, he would have surely written in his own name, as Isaiah and all the other prophets wrote, instead of writing under a feigned name, and putting words into Moses' mouth which he did not speak, and laws he did not give. Good men are not in the habit of telling lies: much less prophets of God. Men do not begin to play cowardly tricks of that kind till after they have lost faith in the *living* God, and got to believe that God was with their forefathers, but is not with them. A Jew of the time of the Apocrypha, or of the time of our Lord, might have done such a thing, because he had lost faith in the living God; but then his work would have been of a very different kind from this noble and heart-stirring book. For the pith and marrow, the essence and life of Deuteronomy is, that it is full of faith in the living God; and for that very reason I am going to speak to you to-day.

For the rest, whether Moses wrote the book down, and put it together in the shape in which we now have it, we shall never be able to tell. The several orations may have been put together into one book. Alterations may have crept in by the carelessness of copiers; sentences may have been added to it by later prophets—as, of course, the grand account of Moses' death, which probably was at first the beginning of the book of Joshua.

And beyond that we need know nothing—even if we need know that.

There the book is ; and people, if they be wise, will, instead of trying to pick it to pieces, read and study it in fear and trembling, that the curses pronounced in it may *not* come, and the blessings pronounced in it may come upon this English land.

Now these Jews were to worship and obey Jehovah, the one true God, and him only.

And why?

Why, indeed ? You *must* understand why, or you will never understand this book of Deuteronomy or any part of the Old Testament, and if you do not, then you will understand very little, if anything, of the New.

You must understand that this was not to be a mere matter of *religion* with the old Jews, this trusting and obeying the true God. Indeed, the word religion, so far as I know, is never mentioned once in the Old Testament at all. By religion we now mean some plan of believing and obeying God, which will save our souls after we die. But Moses said nothing to the Jews about that. He never even anywhere told them that they would live again after this life. We do not know the reason of that. But we may suppose that he knew best. And as we believe that God sent him, we must believe that God knew best also; and that he thought it good for these Jews not to be told too much about the next life; perhaps for fear that they should forget that God was the living God; the God of now, as well as of here-after; the God of this life, as well as of the life to come. My friends, I sometimes think we need putting in mind of that in these days as much as those old Jews did.

However that may be, what Moses promised these Jews, if they trusted in the living God, was that they should be a great nation, they and their children after them; that they should drive out the Canaanites before them; that they should conquer their enemies, and that a thousand should flee before one of them; that they should be blessed in their crops, their orchards, their gardens; that they should have none of the evil diseases of Egypt; that there should be none barren among them, or among their cattle. In a word, that they should be thoroughly and always a strong, happy, prosperous people.

This is what God promised them by Moses, and nothing else; and therefore this is what we must think about, and see whether it has anything to do with us, when we read the book of Deuteronomy, and nothing else.

On the other hand, God warned them by the mouth of Moses that if they forgot the Lord God, and went and worshipped the things round them, men or beasts, or sun and moon and stars, then poverty, misery, and ruin of every kind would surely fall upon them.

And that this last was no empty threat is proved by the plain facts of their sacred history. For they *did* forget God, and worshipped Baalim, the sun, moon, and stars; and ruin of every kind *did* come upon them, till they were carried away captive to Babylon. And this we must think of when we read the book of Deuteronomy, and nothing else.

If they wished to prosper, they were to know and consider in their hearts that Jehovah was God, and there was none else. Yes—this was the continual thought which a true Jew was to have. The thought of a God who was *his* God; the God of his fathers before him, and the God of his children after him; the God of the whole nation of the Jews, throughout all their generations.

But not their God only. No. The God of the Gentiles also, of all the nations upon the earth.

He was to believe that his God alone, of all the gods of the nations, was the true and only God, who had made all nations, and appointed them their times and the bounds of their habitations.

We cannot understand now, in these happier days, all that that meant ; all the strength and comfort, all the godly fear, the feeling of solemn responsibility which that thought ought to have given, and did give to the Jews—that they were the people of Jehovah, the one true God.

For you must remember that all the nations round them then, and all the great heathen nations afterwards, were, as far as we know, the people of some god or other. Religion and politics were with them one and the same thing. They had some god, or gods, whom they looked to as the head or king of their nation, who had a special favour to them, and would bless and prosper them according as they showed him special reverence, and after that god the whole nation was often named.

The Ammonites' god was Ammon, the hidden god, the lord of their sheep and cattle. The Zidonians had Ashtoreth, the moon. The Phœnicians worshipped Moloch, the fire. Many of the Canaanites worshipped Baal, the lord, or Baalim, the lords—the sun, moon, and stars. The Philistines afterwards (for we read nothing of Philistines in Moses' time) worshipped Dagon, the fish-god, and so forth. The Egyptians had gods without number—gods invented out of beasts, and birds, and the fruits of the earth, and the season, and the weather, and the sun and moon and stars. Each class and trade, from the highest to the lowest, and each city and town throughout the land seems to have had its special god, who was worshipped there, and expected to take care of that particular class of men or that particular place.

What a thought it must have been for the Jews—all these people have their gods, but they are all wrong. We have the *right* God ; the only true God. They are the people of this god, or of that ; we are the people of the one true God. They look to many gods ; we look to the one God, who made all things, and beside whom there is none else. They look to one god to bless them in one thing, and another in another ; one to send them sunshine, one to send them fruitful seasons, one to prosper their crops, another their flocks and herds, and so forth. We look to one God to do all these things for us, because he is Lord of all at once, and has made all.

Therefore we need not fear the gods of the heathen, or cry to any of them, even in our utmost distress ; for we belong to him who is before all gods, the God of gods, of whom it is written, 'Worship him, all ye gods ;' and 'It is the Lord who made the heaven and the earth, the sea and all that therein is.   Him only shalt thou worship, and him only shalt thou serve.'   If we obey him, and keep his commandments ; if we trust in him, utterly, through good fortune and through bad —then we must prosper in peace and war, we and our children after us ; because our prosperity is grounded on the real truth, and that of the heathen on a lie ; and all that the heathen expect their false gods to do for them, one here and another there, all that, the one real God will do for us, himself alone.

Do you not see what a power and courage that thought must have given to the Jews ? Do you not see how worshipping God, and loving God, and serving God, must have been a very different, a much deeper, and a truly holier matter to them than the miserable selfish thing which is miscalled religion by too many people now-a-days, by which a man hopes to creep out of this world into heaven all by himself, without any real care or love for his fellow-creatures, or those he leaves behind him?

No. An old Jew's faith in God, and obedience to God, was part of his family life, part of his politics, part of his patriotism. If he obeyed God, and clave earnestly to God, then a blessing would come on him in the field and in the house, on his crops and on his cattle, going out and coming in; and on his children and his children's children to a thousand generations. He would be helping, if he obeyed and trusted God, to advance his country's prosperity; to insure her success in war and peace, to raise the name and fame of the Jewish people among all the nations round, that all might say, 'Surely this great nation is a wise and an understanding people.'

Thus the duty he owed to God was not merely a duty which he owed his own conscience or his own soul; it was a duty which he owed to his family, to his kindred, to his country. It was not merely an opinion that there was one God and not two; it was a belief that the one and only true God was protecting him, teaching him, inspiring him and all his nation. That the true God would teach their hands to war and their fingers to fight. That the true God would cause their folds to be full of sheep. That their valleys should stand rich with corn, that they should laugh and sing. That the true God would enable them to sit every man under his own vine and his own fig-tree, and eat the labour of his hands, he and his children after him to perpetual generations.

This was the message and teaching which God gave these Jews. It is very different from what many people now-a-days would have given them, if they had had the ordering of the matter, and the making of those slaves into a free nation. But perhaps there is one proof that God *did* give it them, and that the Bible speaks truth, when it says that not man, but God gave them their law.

No doubt man would have done it differently. But God's ways are not as man's ways, nor God's thoughts as man's thoughts.

And God's ways have proved themselves to be the right ways. His purpose has come to pass. This little nation of the Jews, inhabiting a country not as large as Wales, without sea-port towns and commerce, without colonies or conquests— and at last, for its own sins, conquered itself, and scattered abroad over the whole civilized world—has taught the whole civilized world, has converted the whole civilized world, has influenced all the good and all the wise unto this day so enormously, that the world has actually gone beyond them, and become Christian by fully understanding their teaching and their Bible, while they have remained mere Jews by not fully understanding it.   Truly, if that is not a proof that God revealed something to the Jews which they never found out for themselves, which was too great for them to understand, which was God's boundless message and not any narrow message of man's invention—if that does not prove it, I say—I know not what proof men would have.

But now I have told you that God bade these Jews to look for blessings in *this* life, and blessings on their whole nation, and on their children after them, if they obeyed and served him.   Does God *not* bid us to look for any such blessings ?   The Jews were to be blessed in *this* world.   Are we only to be blessed in the next ?

To that the Seventh Article of our Church gives a plain and positive answer.   For it says that those are not to be heard who pretend that the old Fathers, *i.e.* Moses and the Prophets, looked only for transitory promises—*i.e.* for promises which would pass away.   No.   They looked for eternal promises which could not pass away, because they were according to the eternal laws of God, which stand good both for this world and for all worlds ; for this life and for the life everlasting.

Yes, my friends, settle in your hearts that the book of Deuteronomy is meant for you, and for all the nations upon earth, as much as for the old Jews. That its promises and warnings are to you and to your children as surely as they were to the old Jews. Ay, that they are meant for every nation that is, or ever was, or ever will be upon earth. If you would prosper on the earth, fear God and keep his commandments ; and know and consider it in your heart that the Lord Jesus Christ he is God in heaven above and on the earth beneath : there is none else. He it is who gives grace and honour. He it is who delivers us out of the hands of our enemies. He it is who blesses the fruit of the womb, and the fruit of the flock, and the fruit of the garden and the field. He is the living God, in whom this world, as well as the world to come, lives and moves and has its being; and only by obeying his laws can man prosper, he and his children after him, upon this earth of God.

SERMON XVI.

NATIONAL WEALTH.

(Fifth Sunday after Easter.)

DEUT. viii. 11—18.

Beware that thou forget not the Lord thy God, in not keeping his commandments, and his judgments, and his statutes, which I command thee this day: lest when thou hast eaten and art full, and hast built goodly houses, and dwelt therein; and when thy herds and thy flocks multiply, and thy silver and thy gold is multiplied, and all that thou hast is multiplied; then thine heart be lifted up, and thou forget the Lord thy God, which brought thee forth out of the land of Egypt, from the house of bondage; who led thee through that great and terrible wilderness, wherein were fiery serpents, and scorpions, and drought, where there was no water; who brought thee forth water out of the rock of flint; who fed thee in the wilderness with manna, which thy fathers knew not, that he might humble thee and that he might prove thee, to do thee good at thy latter end: and thou say in thine heart, My power and the might of mine hand hath gotten me this wealth. But thou shalt remember the Lord thy God: for it is he that giveth thee power to get wealth, that he may establish his covenant which he sware unto thy fathers, as it is this day.

I TOLD you before that the book of Deuteronomy was the foundation of all sound politics —as one would expect it to be, if its author were Moses, the greatest lawgiver whom the world ever saw. But here, in this lesson, is a proof of the truth of what I said. For here, in the text, is Moses' answer to the first great question in politics, What makes a nation prosperous?

To that wise men have always answered, as Moses answered, 'Good government; government according to the laws of God.' That alone makes a nation prosperous.

But the multitude—who are not wise men, nor likely to be for some time to come—give a different answer. They say, 'What makes a nation prosperous is its wealth. If Britain be only *rich*, then she must be safe and right.'

To which Moses, being a wise lawgiver, and having, moreover, in him the Spirit of the Lord who knoweth what is in man, makes a reasonable, liberal, humane answer.

Moses does not deny that wealth is a good thing. He does not bid them not try to be rich. He takes for granted that they will grow rich; that the national fruit of their good government will be that they will increase in cattle and in crops and in money, and in all which makes an agricultural people rich.

He takes for granted, I say, that these Jews will grow very rich; but he warns them that their riches, like all other earthly things, may be a curse or a blessing to them. Nay, that they are not good in themselves, but mere tools which may be used for good or for evil. He warns them of a very great danger that riches will bring on them. And herein he shows his knowledge of the human heart; for it is a certain fact that whenever any nation has prospered, and their flocks and herds, and silver and gold, all that they had, have multiplied, then they have, as Moses warned the Jews, forgotten the Lord their God, and said, ' My power and the might of my hand hath gotten me this wealth.'

And it is true, also, that whenever any nation has begun to say that, they have fallen into confusion and misery, and sometimes into utter ruin, till they repented, and turned and remembered the Lord their God, and found out that the strength of a nation did not consist in riches, but in *virtue*. For it is he that giveth the power to get wealth. He gives it in two ways: First, God gives the raw material ; secondly, he gives the wit to use it.

You will all agree that God gives the first ; that he gives the soil, the timber, the fisheries, the coal, the iron.

Do you believe it ? I hope and trust that you

do. But I fear that now-a-days many do not; for they boast of the resources of Britain as if we ourselves had made Britain, and not Almighty God; as if we had put the coal and the iron into the rocks, and not Almighty God ages before we were born.

And if they will not say that openly, at least they will say, 'But the coal, and iron, and all other raw material would have been useless, if it had not been for the genius and energy of the British race.'

Of course not. But who gave them that genius and energy? Who gave them the wit to find the coal and iron?

God; and God gave it to us when we needed it, and not before.

Think of this, I beseech you; for it is true, and wonderful, and a thing of which I may say, 'Come, and I will reason with you of the righteous acts of the Lord.'

Men say, 'As long as England is ahead of the world in coal and iron she may defy the world.' I do not believe it; for if she became a wicked nation all the coal and iron in the universe would not keep her from being ruined.

But even if it were true, which it is not, that

the strength of Britain lies in coal and iron, and not in British hearts, what right have we to boast of coal and iron?

Did our forefathers know of them when they came into this land? Did they come after coal and iron?

Not they. They came here to settle as small yeomen; to till miserable little patches of corn, of which we should be now ashamed, and to feed cattle on the moors, and swine in the forests— and that was all they looked to. Then they found that there was iron, principally down south, in Sussex and Surrey; and they worked it, clumsily enough, with charcoal; and for more than twelve hundred years they were here in England, with no notion of the boundless wealth in iron and coal lying together in the same rocks which God had provided for them; or if they did guess at it, they could not use it, because they could not work deep mines, being unable to pump out the water; for God had not opened their eyes and shown them how to do it.

But just when it was wanted, God did show them. About the middle of the last century the iron in the Weald was all but worked out; the charcoal wood was getting scarcer and scarcer, and there was every chance that England, instead of being ahead of all nations in iron, would have fallen behind other nations; and then where should we have been now?

But, just about one hundred years ago, it pleased God to open the eyes of certain men, and they invented steam-engines. Then they could pump the mines, then they could discover and use the vast riches of our coal-mines. Then, too, sprung up a thousand useful arts and manufactures; while the land, not being wanted for charcoal and firewood, as of old, could be cleared of wood, and thousands of acres set free to grow corn. Population, which had been all but standing still, without increasing, has now more than doubled, and wealth inestimable has come to this generation, of which our forefathers never dreamed.

Now what have we to boast of in that? What, save to confess ourselves a very stupid race, who for twelve hundred years could not discover, or at least use the boundless wealth which God had given us, because we had not wit enough to invent so simple a thing as a steam-engine.

All we should do, instead of boasting, is to bless God that he revealed to us just what we needed, and at the very time at which we needed it, and confess that it is *he* that giveth us power to get wealth. It is he that hath made us, and not we ourselves.

Look again at another case, even more extraordinary, which has happened during our own times—indeed within the last ten years—the discovery of gold in Australia.

There had been rumours and whispers of gold for years before ; and yet no one looked for gold, cared for it, hardly believed in it. God had dulled their understanding and blinded their eyes for some good purpose of his own. That is what the Bible would have said of such a matter, and that is what we should say.

And at last some man finds lying out upon the downs a huge lump of gold—by accident (as men call it ; by the special providence of God, as they ought to call it) ; and at that every one starts up and awakes, and begins looking for gold. And now that their eyes are opened, behold! the gold is everywhere. Not merely in lonely forests and unexplored mountains, but on farms where the sheep have been pastured for years past ; ay, even Melbourne streets were full of gold, under the feet of the passengers and the wheels of the carriages ; there had the gold been all along, but men could not see it till God opened their eyes. Verily, verily, God is great, and man is small. I do not say that this was a miracle in the common meaning of the word; but I do say that this was a striking instance of that everlasting and special providence of the living God, who ordereth all things in heaven and earth, from the rise of a nation to the fall of a sparrow; and does so, not by breaking his own laws, but by making his laws work exactly as he will, when he will, and where he will; and I say that it is a fresh proof of the great saying, that no man can see a thing unless God shows it to him. For it is the Lord who gives us power to get wealth. It is he that hath made us, and not we ourselves; and in him we live and move, and have our being.

This, then, was what Moses commanded—to remember that they owed all to God. What they had, they had of God's free gift. What they were, they were by God's free grace. Therefore they were not to boast of themselves, their numbers, their wealth, their armies, their fair and fertile land. They were to make their boast of God, and of God's goodness.

He that gloried was to glory in the Lord, and confess that a Syrian ready to perish was their father Jacob, when the Lord had mercy on him, and made him the head of a great tribe, and the father of a great nation; that not themselves, but God had brought them out of Egypt with signs and wonders; that they got not the land in possession by their own bow, neither was it their own sword that helped them, but that God had driven out before them nations greater and mightier than they.

This they were to remember, because it was true. And this we are to remember, because it is more or less true of us. God has put us where we are. God has made of us a great nation; God has discovered to us the immense riches of this land. It is he that hath made us, and not we ourselves.

But more. You will see that Moses warns them that if they forget God, the Lord who brought them out of the land of Egypt, they would go after other gods.

He cannot part the two things. If they forget that God brought them out of Egypt, they will turn to idolatry, and so end in ruin.

Now why was this?

Why should not the Jews have gone on worshipping one God, even if they had forgotten that he brought them out of the land of Egypt?

Some people now-a-days think that they would, and that they might have very well been what is called Monotheists, without believing all the story of the signs and wonders in Egypt, and the passage of the Red Sea, and the giving of the law to Moses.

Such men may be very learned; but there is one thing of which they know very little, and that is, human nature. Moses knew human nature; and he knew that if men forgot that God was the living God, the acting God, who had helped them once, and was helping them always, and only believed about there being one God far away in heaven, and not two, that *that* sort of dead faith in a dead God would never keep them from idols. They would want gods who *would* help them, who *would* hear their prayers, to whom they could feel gratitude and trust; and they would invent them for themselves, and begin to worship things in the heavens above, and the earth beneath, because they had forgotten their true friend and helper, the living God.

And so shall we. If we forget that God is the living God, who brought our forefathers into this land ; who has revealed to us the wealth of it step by step, as we needed it; who is helping and blessing us now, every day and all the year round —then we shall begin worshipping other gods.

I do not mean that we shall worship idols, though I do not see why our children's children should not do so a few hundred years hence if we teach them to forget the living God. There are too many Christians at this day who worship saints, and idols of wood and stone; and so may our descendants do—or do even worse.

But we ourselves shall begin—indeed we are doing it too much already—worshipping the so-called laws of nature, instead of God who made the laws, and so honouring the creature above the creator; or else we shall worship the pomps and vanities of this world, pride and power, money and pleasure, and say in our hearts, 'These are our only gods which can help us—these' must we obey.' Which if we do, this land of England will come to ruin and shame, as surely as did the land of Israel in old time.

If we do not believe in the living God, we shall believe in something worse than even a dead god. For in a dead god—a god who does nothing, but lets mankind and the world go their own way—no man nor nation ever will care to believe.

And now, my dear friends, remember that a

nation is, after all, only the people in that nation: you, and I, and our neighbours, and our neighbours' neighbours, and so forth; and that therefore, in as far as we are wrong, we do our worst to make the British nation wrong. If we give way to ungodly pride and self-sufficiency, then we are injuring ourselves; and not only that, but injuring our neighbours and our children after us, as far as we can. And therefore our duty is, if we wish well to our nation, not to judge our neighbour, nor our neighbour's neighbour, but to judge ourselves.

If we go on trusting in ourselves rather than God; if we keep within us the hard self-sufficient spirit, and boast to ourselves (though we may be ashamed to boast to our neighbours), 'My power and the strength of my hands have got me this and that;' and in fact live under the notion, which too many have, that we could do very well without God's help if God would let us alone—then we are heaping up ruin and shame for ourselves and for our children after us. Ruin and shame, I say. We are apt to forget how easy and common it is for God to turn the wisdom of men into folly; to frustrate the tokens of the liars, and make the prophets mad. How men blow great bubbles, and

God bursts them with the slightest touch. How, when all seems well, and men cry peace and safety, sudden destruction comes upon them unawares. How, when men say, 'Soul, take thine ease, eat, drink, and be merry; thou hast much goods laid up for many years,' God answers, 'Thou fool, this night shall thy soul be required of thee.'

My friends, we see God doing thus in these very days by great nations, by great branches of industry. Look at the American war, look at the Manchester cotton famine, and see how God can confound the strong and cunning, and blind their eyes to the ruin which is coming till it is come in all its might. And then think, If it be so easy for him to confound such as them, is it less easy for him to confound you and me, if we begin to fancy that we can do without him, and ask, 'Doth God perceive it? Or is there knowledge in the Most High? We are they that ought to speak. Who is Lord over us?'

Yes, in this sense God is indeed a jealous God, who will not give his honour to another. And a blessed thing for men it is that God *is* a jealous God, that he *will* punish us for trusting in anything but him—will punish us for trusting ih ourselves, or in our wisdom, or in wealth, or in science, or in armies and navies, or in constitutions and laws; in anything, in short, save the living God.

For if he left us alone to go our own way without trusting or fearing him, we should surely go down and down (as the Chinese seem to have gone down), generation after generation, till we became only a mere cunning and spiteful sort of animals, hateful and hating one another. But when we are chastened for our folly, we are chastened by him that we may be partakers of his holiness; that we may be his children, looking up to him as our father, from whom comes every good and perfect gift; the Father of Lights, with whom is no variableness or shadow of turning; and who therefore will and can give us, his children, light, more and more to understand those his invariable and eternal laws, by which he has made earth and heaven; who has given us his Son Jesus Christ our Lord, and will with him likewise freely give us all things.

SERMON XVII.

THE GOD OF THE RAIN.

(Fifth Sunday after Easter.)

DEUT. xi. 11, 12.

The land, whither ye go to possess it, is a land of hills and
valleys, and drinketh water of the rain of heaven. A land
which the Lord thy God careth for: the eyes of the Lord
thy God are always upon it, from the beginning of the year,
even unto the end of the year.

I TOLD you, when I spoke of the earthquakes
of the Holy Land, that it seems as if God
had meant specially to train that strange people
the Jews, by putting them into a country where
they *must* trust him, or become cowards and
helpless; that so they might learn not to fear
the powers of Nature which the heathen worshipped, but to fear him the living God.

In this chapter is another instance of the same.
They were to be an agricultural people. Their
very worship was (if you can understand such

a thing now-a-days) to be agricultural. Pentecost was a feast of the first-fruits of the harvest. The Feast of Tabernacles was a great national harvest home. The Passover itself, though not at first an agricultural festival, became one by the waving of the Paschal sheaf, which gave permission to the people to begin their spring-harvest —so thoroughly were they to be an agricultural and cattle-feeding people. They were going into a good land, a land of milk and honey and oil olive; a land of vines and figs and pomegranates; a rich land; but a most uncertain land—a land which might yield a splendid crop one year, and be almost barren the next.

It was not as the land of Egypt—a land which was, humanly speaking, sure to be fertile, because always supplied with water, brought out of the Nile by dykes and channels which spread in a network over every field, and where—as I believe is done now—the labourer turned the water from one land to the other simply by moving the earth with his foot.

It was a mountain land, a land of hills and valleys, and drank water of the rain of heaven; a land of fountains of water, which required to be fed continually by the rain. In that hot climate it depended entirely on God's providence from week to week whether a crop could grow.

Therefore it was a land which the Lord cared for—a land which needed his special help, and it had it. 'The eyes of the Lord God were always upon it, from the beginning of the year unto the end of the year.'

Beautiful, simple, noble, true words—deeper than all the learned words, however true they may be (and true they are, and to be listened to with respect), which men talk about the laws of Nature and of weather. Who would change them for all the scientific phrases in the world?

The eyes of the Lord were upon the land. It needed his care; and therefore his care it had.

Therefore the Jew was to understand from his first entry into the land, that his prosperity depended utterly on God. The laws of weather, by which the rain comes up off the sea, were unknown to him. They are all but unknown to us now. But they were known to God. Not a drop could fall without his providence and will; and therefore they were utterly in his power.

'And it shall come to pass, if ye shall hearken diligently unto my commandments which I command you this day, to love the Lord your God, and to serve him with all your heart and with all your soul, that I will give you the rain of your land in his due season, the first rain and the latter rain, that thou mayest gather in thy corn, and thy wine, and thine oil. And I will send grass in thy fields for thy cattle, that thou mayest eat and be full. Take heed to yourselves, that your heart be not deceived, and ye turn aside and serve other gods, and worship them ; and then the Lord's wrath be kindled against you, and he shut up the heaven, that there be no rain, and that the land yield not her fruit ; and lest ye perish quickly from off the good land which the Lord giveth you.'

Now the Bible story is, that this warning came true. More than once we read of drought—long, and severe, and ruinous. In one famous case, there was no rain for three years ; and Ahab has to go out to search through the land for a scrap of pasture. 'Peradventure we shall find grass enough to save the horses and mules alive.'

And most distinctly does the Bible say that these droughts came at times when the Jews had fallen into idolatry, and profligacy therewith. That is the Scripture account. And if you believe in the living God, whose providence ordereth

all things in heaven and earth, that account will
seem reasonable and credible to you.

What special means God used to bring about
these great droughts we cannot know, any more
than we can know why a storm or a shower
should come one week and not another. And
we need not know. God made the world, and
God governs the world, and that is enough for us.

Be that as it may, Moses goes down to the very
root and ground and true cause of the riches of
the land, and of the rainfall, and of the prosperity
of the Jews, and of the prosperity of any living
nation on earth, when he says, 'Therefore shall
ye lay up these my words in your heart and in
your soul, and bind them for a sign upon your
hand, that they may be as frontlets between your
eyes.'

'Ye shall lay up these my words in your heart
and your soul, and teach them your children when
thou sittest in thine house and when thou walkest
by the way, when thou liest down and when thou
risest up.' That is, thou shalt believe continually
in a living God—a God who is working everywhere at every moment, about thy path and about
thy bed, and spying out all thy ways; and not
only about thee, but about all that thou seest.

From him comes alike rain and sunshine; from him comes the life of man; from him comes all which makes it possible for man to live upon the earth.

And it is a plain fact that the Jews for a long time did believe this—at least the prophets, psalmists and good men among them—to the most intense degree; to a degree in which perhaps no nation has believed it since. With them God is everything, and man nothing. Man finds out nothing: God reveals it to him. Man's intellect does nothing: the Spirit of God gives him understanding to do it—even, says Isaiah, understanding to plough, and to sow, and to reap his crops in due season. It is the Spirit of God, according to the prophets and psalmists, which makes the difference between a man and a beast. But upon the beasts too, and the green things of the earth, and on all nature, the Spirit of God works. He is the Lord and giver of life. Take only those four Psalms, the 8th, 18th, 29th, 104th, and learn from them what the old Jews thought of this wonderful world in which we live.

'These all wait upon thee'—all living things by land and sea—'that thou mayest give them meat in due season. When thou givest it them they gather it. When thou openest thy hand they are filled with good. When thou hidest thy face they are troubled. When thou takest away their breath they die, and are turned again to their dust. When thou lettest thy breath go forth they shall be made, and thou shalt renew the face of the earth.'

So again, in the world of man, God is the living Judge, the living overlooker, rewarder, punisher of every man, not only in the life to come, but in this life. His providence is a special providence. But not such a poor special providence as men are too apt to dream of now-a-days, which interferes only now and then on some great occasion, or on behalf of some very favoured persons, but a special providence looking after every special act of man, and of the whole universe, from the fall of a sparrow to the fall of an empire.

And it is this intense faith in the living God, which can only come by the inspiration of the Spirit of God, which proves the old Testament to be truly inspired. This it is which makes it different from all books in the world. This it is, I hold, which marks the canon of Scripture. For in the Apocrypha—true, noble, and good as most of it is—you do not find the same intense faith in the living God, or anything to be compared there-with ; and that for the simple reason that the Jews, at the time the Apocrypha was written, were losing that faith very fast. They felt them-selves that there was an immense difference be-tween anything that they could write and what the old psalmists and prophets had written. They felt that they could not write Scripture. All they could do was to write commentaries about it, and to carry out in their own fashion Moses' command, 'Thou shalt bind my words for a sign upon your hands, and they shall be as frontlets between your eyes, and thou shalt write them upon the door-posts of thine house.' They were right in that ; but as they lost faith in the living God, they began to observe the command in the letter, and neglect it in the spirit.

You know—some of you, at least—how these words were misused afterwards; how the scribes and the Pharisees, in their zeal to carry out the letter of the law, went about with texts of Scrip-ture on their foreheads, and wrists, and the hems of their robes, enlarging their phylacteries, as our Lord said of them. But all the time they did not understand the texts, or love them, or get any good from them ; but only made them excuses

for hating and scoffing at the rest of the world.
They had them written only on their foreheads,
not on their hearts—an outside and not an inside
religion. They had lost all faith in the living
God. God had spoken, of course, to their forefathers; but they could not believe that he was
speaking to them—not even when he spoke by
his only begotten Son, the brightness of his glory,
and the express image of his person. God, so
they held, had finished his teaching when Malachi
uttered his last prophecy. And now it was for
them to teach, and expound the law at second-
hand. There could be no more prophets, no
more revelation; and when one came and spoke
with authority, at first hand, out of the depth of
his own heart, he was to be persecuted, stoned,
crucified. No. They had the key of knowledge;
and no man could enter in, unless they chose to
open the door. Nothing new could be true. John
the Baptist came neither eating nor drinking, and
they said, 'He hath a devil.' The Son of Man
came eating and drinking, and they said, 'Behold
a gluttonous man and a wine-bibber, a friend of
publicans and sinners.' And meanwhile the poor,
the ignorant, those whose hearts were really in
earnest, were looking out for a prophet and a

deliverer—often going after false prophets, with Theudas and Barcochab, into the wilderness; but going, too, to be baptized with the baptism of John, and crowding in thousands to hear our Lord preach to them of the living God of whom Moses had preached of old; while the scribes and Pharisees sat at home, wrapped up in their narrow, shallow book-divinity, and said, 'This people, who knoweth not the law, is accursed.' Nothing new could be true. It must be put down, persecuted down, lest the Romans should come and take away their place and nation.

But they did not succeed. Our Lord and his truth, whom they crucified and buried, rose again the third day and conquered; and the Romans came after all, and took away their place and nation. And so they failed, as all will fail, who will not believe in the living God.

My friends, all these things were written for our example. As it was then, so may it be again.

There may come a time in this land when people shall profess to worship the word of God; and yet, like those old scribes, make it of none effect by their own commandments and traditions. When they shall command men, like the scribes, to honour every word and letter of the Bible, and yet forbid them to take the Bible simply and literally as it stands, but only their interpretation of the Bible; when they shall say, with the scribes, 'Nothing new can be true. God taught the Apostles, and therefore he is not teaching us. God worked miracles of old; but whosoever thinks that God is working miracles now is a Pantheist and a blasphemer. God taught men of old the thing which they knew not; but whosoever dares to say that he does so now is bringing heresy and false doctrine, and undermining the Christian faith by science falsely so called.'

And all because they have lost all faith in the living God—the ever-working, ever-teaching, ever-inspiring, ever-governing God whom our Lord Jesus Christ revealed to men; in whom the Apostles, and the Fathers, and the great middle-age Schoolmen, and the Reformers believed, and therefore learned more and more, and taught men more and more concerning God and the dealings of God, as time went on.

And then, when they see ignorant people running after quacks and impostors, spirit-rappers and table-turners, St. Simonians and Mormons, and false prophets of every kind, they will have nothing to say but 'This people which knoweth not the law is accursed.' While when they see anything like new truth, or new teaching from God appear, instead of welcoming the light, and going to meet the light, and accepting the light, they will say, 'What shall we do? For all men will believe on him, and then the powers of this world will come and take away our station and our order?' As if Christ could not take better care of his Church for which he died than they can in his stead! And so they will persecute God's servants, in the name of God, and call upon the law to put down by force the men whom they cannot put down by reason.

From ever falling into that state of stupid lip-belief, and outward religion, and loss of faith in the living God: Good Lord, deliver us.

From all blindness of heart; from pride, vain-glory, and hypocrisy; from envy, hatred, and malice, and all uncharitableness: Good Lord, deliver us.

From all false doctrine, heresy, and schism; from hardness of heart and contempt of thy word and commandment: Good Lord, deliver us.

For if people ever fall into that frame of mind (as did the scribes and Pharisees), and the good

Lord do not deliver them from it, it will surely happen to them as it is written in the Bible.

The powers of this world will come and take away their place, and their power, and their station : but meanwhile the truth which they think that they have stifled will rise again, for Christ, who is the truth, will raise it again ; and it shall conquer and leaven the hearts of men till all be leavened ; and while the scribes and Pharisees shall be cast into the outer darkness of discontented and hopeless bigotry, the kingdoms of the world, which they fancied were the devil's dominion, shall become the kingdoms of God and of his Christ, and be adopted into that holy and ever-growing Church, of which it is written, that the gates of hell shall not prevail against it, for in it is the Spirit of God to lead it into all truth.

To which blessed end may God bring us, and our children after us.   Amen.

SERMON XVIII.

THE DEATH OF MOSES.

(First Sunday after Trinity.)

DEUT. xxxiv. 5, 6.

So Moses the servant of the Lord died there in the land of Moab,
according to the word of the Lord. And he buried him in a
valley in the land of Moab, over against Beth-peor; but no man
knoweth of his sepulchre unto this day.

SOME might regret that the last three chapters
of Deuteronomy are not read among our Sunday lessons. There was not, however, room for
them; and I do not doubt that those who chose
our lessons knew better than I what chapters they
ought to choose. We may, however, read them
for ourselves, not only in the daily lessons, but
as often as we choose. And well worth reading
they are.

For I know of no stronger proof of the truth
of the book of Deuteronomy, and of the whole

Pentateuch, than its ending so differently from what we should have expected, or indeed wished. If things went in this world, as they do in novels and fables, according to man's notion of what is right and good, then Moses and his history would have had a very different ending.

And if the story of Moses had been of man's invention, we should have heard—I think, from what we know of the fables, 'myths' as they call them now, which nations have invented about themselves, and their own early history, we may guess fairly what we should have heard—how Moses brought the Jews into the land of Canaan, and established his laws, and reigned over them, and died in honour and great glory—if he died at all, and was not taken up into the skies, and changed into a star, or into a god; and how he was buried with great pomp; and how his sepulchre did remain among the Jews until that day; and probably how men worshipped at it, and miracles were worked at it, and so forth.

Also, we should have heard how, as soon as the Israelites came into the land of Canaan, they began forthwith to serve the Lord with all their heart and soul, as they never did afterwards, and to keep Moses' law, while it was yet fresh in their minds, more exactly than ever they did after-wards; and in short, we should have had one of those stories of a 'golden age,' a 'good old time,' a pattern-time of early purity and devotion, of which nations and Churches, of all tongues and all creeds, have been so ready to dream in their own case; and which they have used, not altogether ill, to rebuke vice in their own day, by saying, 'Look how perfect your forefathers were. Look how you, their unworthy children, have fallen from their faith and their virtue.'

This, I think, is what we should have been told if the Pentateuch had been the invention of man. This is exactly what we are *not* told; but, on the contrary, the very opposite.

What we are told is disappointing, sad, gloomy, full of dark fears and warnings about what the Jews will be and what they will have to endure. But it is far more true to human nature, and to the facts which we see in the world about us, than any story of a good old time would have been.

They are still wandering in the land of Moab, when the time draws near when Moses must die. He is a hundred and twenty years old, but hale and vigorous still. His eye is not dim, nor his natural force abated. But the Lord has told him that his death is near. He gives the command of the army of Israel to Joshua the son of Nun, and then he speaks his last words.

Songs they are, dark and rugged, like all the higher Hebrew poetry; but, like it, full of the very Spirit of God—the Spirit of wisdom and understanding, the Spirit of faith and of the fear of the Lord.

There are three of these songs which seem to belong to those last days of his.

The Prayer of Moses the man of God—which is our 90th Psalm, our burial Psalm. We all know the sadness of that Psalm; its weariness, as of one who had laboured long, and would fain be at rest; its confession of man's frailty—fading away suddenly like the grass; its confession of God's strength, God from everlasting, before the mountains were brought forth; its eternal gospel of hope and comfort, that the strength of God takes pity on the weakness of man, 'Lord, thou hast been our refuge, from one generation to another.'

Then comes the Song of the Rock—the song of which (it seems) the Lord said to him, 'Write this song, and teach it the children of Israel, that it may be a witness for me against them.'

And so Moses writes; and seemingly before all the congregation of Israel, according to the custom of those times, he chants his death-song, the Song of the Rock. It is such a song as we should expect from him. God is the Rock. He was thinking, it may be, of the everlasting rocks of Sinai, where God had appeared to him of old. But God is the true, everlasting Rock, on which all things rest; the Eternal, the Self-existent, the I Am, whom he was sent to preach to men. But he is a good and righteous God likewise. His work is perfect. 'A God of truth, and without iniquity, just and right is he.'

In him Moses can trust, but not in the children of Israel; they are a perverse and crooked generation, who have waxen fat and kicked. God has done all for them, but they will not obey him. Even in the wilderness they have worshipped strange gods, and sacrificed to devils, not to God; and so they will do after Moses is gone; and then on them will come all the curses of which he has so often warned them. 'The sword without, and terror within, shall destroy both the young man and the virgin, the suckling also with the man of gray hairs. O that they were wise, that they understood this, that they would consider their latter end! How 'should one chase a thousand; and two put ten thousand to flight?' What a people they might be, and what a future there is before them, if they would but be true to God! But they will not. And so Moses' death-song, like his life's wish, ends in disappointment and sadness, and dread of the evils which are coming upon his beloved countrymen.

Lastly, he blesses them, tribe by tribe, in strange and grand words, such as dying men utter, who, looking earnestly across the dark river of death, see further than they ever saw amid the cares and temptations of life. And he blesses them. He will say nothing of them but good. He will speak not of what they will be, but of what they ought to be and can be. But not in their own strength— only in the strength of God. Man is to be nothing to the last; and God is all in all.

'There is none like unto the God of Jeshurun, who rideth upon the heaven in thy help, and in his excellency on the sky. The eternal God is thy refuge, and underneath are the everlasting arms.

'Happy art thou, O Israel: who is like unto thee, O people saved by the Lord, the shield of thy help and who is the sword of thy excellency!

and thine enemies shall be found liars unto thee; and thou shalt tread upon their high places.'

Those are the last words of Moses. Then he goes up into the mountain top, never to return; and the children of Israel are left alone with God and their own souls, to obey and prosper, or disobey and die.

The time of their schooling is past, and their schoolmaster is gone for ever. They are no more to be under a human tutor. They are come to man's estate and man's responsibility, and they are to work out their own fortunes by their own deeds, like every other soul of man.

For Moses himself must not enter into the promised land. In spite of all his faith, his courage, his endurance, his patriotism, he has sinned against God, and he must be punished; and punished, too, in kind—in the very thing which he will feel most deeply, in being shut out from the very happiness on which he has set his heart all along.

He who has brought the Jews to the edge of the promised land must not have the honour and glory of taking them into it. He must have no honour and glory. That must be God's alone. Man must be nothing, and God all in all. Moses

must die in faith, not having received the promises, as many another saint of God has died.

And why? To teach him and the Jews and
us that man *is* nothing, and God is all in all.

Moses had given way to the very temptation
which would beset such a man. He had spoken
unadvisedly with his lips, and said, 'Hear now,
ye rebels, or ye fools, must *we* bring you water
out of this rock?' *We*, and not God. He had
claimed for himself the power and glory of working miracles. The miracles, he thought for a
moment, were his, and not God's. And it may
be that this was not the only time that he had so
sinned. He may naturally have thought that he
had some special power and influence with God.
But be that as it may, the Jews were trained to
believe that the miracles were God's, God's im-
mediate work, and not performed by the wisdom
or sanctity or supernatural power of any saint or
prophet whatsoever. Let the Jews once learn to
give the honour and glory to Moses, and not to
God, and the whole of their strange education
went for nothing. Instead of worshipping God
they would begin to worship saints. Instead of
trusting in God, they would begin to trust in men;
whether on earth or in heaven matters not. If

Moses was to have the honour and glory, the Jews would surely grow into a superstitious, saint-worshipping, miracle-mongering people, and come to ruin and slavery thereby. They were to fear God and nought else. To trust in God and nought else.

So Moses must vanish out of their sight, sadly and mysteriously. All they know of him is, that he is punished for a sin which he committed long ago, as you and I may be. All they know of his death and burial is, that his body was not left foully to the birds of the air and the beasts of the field; for the Lord buried him. They know not how, and did not need to know. And we need not know. Enough for them and for us to know that no dishonour was done to the grand old man; that as he died far away on the lonely mountain top without a child to close his eyes, his last look fixed upon the good land and large which lay spread out below, of entering which he had been dreaming for forty—it may be for more than forty—years. Enough for us to know that the kindly earth received his body again into her bosom, and that the true Moses—the immortal spirit of the man—returned to God who created him, and inspired him, and sustained him to be perhaps the greatest man—save One who was more than man—who ever trod this earth.

So our human feelings, like those of the Jews, are satisfied. But Moses is not to be worshipped by them or by us; no splendid temple is to rise over his bones; no lamps are to burn, or priest to chant round his shrine; no miracles are to be worked by his relics; no man is to invoke his patronage and intercession in their prayers. The people whom he has brought out of Egypt are to be free—free from the slavery of the body, free from the more degrading slavery of the soul.

And so they go on over Jordan to fulfil their strange destiny, to fight their way into the promised land, to root out the Canaanite tribes, whose iniquity was full, whose sins had made them a nuisance not to be suffered on the earth of God. But do they go to establish a golden age; to become a perfect people?

Nothing less. To become, according to the book of Judges, just what Moses foretold—an ignorant, selfish, often profligate and disorderly people, doing each what is right in his own eyes, falling continually into idolatry, civil war, and slavery to the heathens round about. Nothing more shows the truth of this history than its humility, its continual confession of sin, its readiness to confess the ugly truth that the Jews are a foolish, ignorant, unmanageable, lawless, sensual race, stiffnecked and rebellious, always resisting the Holy Spirit. The immense difference between the Old Testament history and that of all other nations is, that it is a history not of their virtues, but of their sins; and a history, on the other hand, of God's punishments and mercies. God in the Old Testament is all, and the Jews are nothing; and one may say that it differs from all other histories in this, that it is not a history of the Jews themselves at all, but a history of God's dealings with them.

If any man chooses to explain that, by saying that the story was all invented by priests and prophets afterwards, to rebuke the people for falling into idolatry, he must have his fancy. Thought is free—for the present, at least—though it is written that for every idle word that men speak, they shall give account at the day of judgment. But one question I must ask, and I am sure that British common sense and British honesty will ask it too: If these prophets were really good men, fearing God, and wishing to make their countrymen fear him likewise, would it not have been a rather strange way of showing that they feared God to tell their countrymen a set of fables and lies? Good men are not in the habit of telling lies now, and never have been ; for no lie is of the truth, or can possibly help the truth in any way ; and all liars have their portion in the lake which burneth with fire and brimstone. And that such men as the prophets of whom we read in the Old Testament did not know that, and therefore invented this history, or invented anything else, is a thing incredible and absurd.

Here we have the Old Testament, an infinitely good book, giving us infinitely good advice and good news, and news too concerning God—God's laws, God's providence, God's dealings, such as we get nowhere else. And shall we believe that this infinitely good book is founded upon falsehood? or that the good men who wrote it could fancy it necessary to stoop to falsehood, and take the devil's tools wherewith to do God's work ? That they may have been imperfectly informed on some points there is no doubt; for the Bible tells us that they were men of like passions with ourselves, and they may not always have been true to the Spirit of God who was teaching them, even as we are not, though he teaches us. They only knew in part and prophesied in part; and now that which is perfect is come, that which is in part is done away; the mystery of Christ was not revealed to them as it has been to us by the holy apostles and prophets of the new dispensation, of which St. Paul says, comparing it with the knowledge which the old Jews had when the gospel came, That the glory of the law had no glory, by reason of the more excellent glory of the gospel. They may, I say, have made slight errors in unimportant matters, though it is far more probable that those errors have crept into the text, as the Scriptures were copied again and again through many centuries by different scribes, of whose perfect good sense and honesty we cannot be certain. But who that really values his Bible cares for them any more than he cares for the spots on the sun which he can find through a telescope? The sun still shines, and gives light to the whole earth, and the Bible still shines, and gives light to every soul of man who will read it in reverence and faith. But that the prophets ever invented, or ever dared to tamper with truth, is a thing not to be believed of men whose writings are plainly, by their own meaning and end, inspired by the Holy Spirit of God.

One more reason—and a reason which to me is unanswerable—for believing, like our forefathers, that the Old Testament is true. The Old Testament, as well as the New, tells us of the 'noble acts' of the Lord—of certain gracious and merciful and just things which the Lord did to the children of Israel. But if that be not true, what follows? That God has not done the noble acts which men thought he had, and therefore that God is not as noble as men thought he was; that men have actually fancied for themselves a better God than the God who exists already.

Absurd.

Absurd, truly; and if you choose to call it by a harder name still, you have a right to do so.

Do not you think that God must be better, not worse; more generous, not less ; more condescending, not less ; more just, not less ; more helpful, not less, than man can fancy or describe? Are not the riches of Christ unsearchable, and the mercies of the Lord boundless? Is he not able and willing to do exceeding abundantly beyond all that we can ask or think? Did not even St. Paul say that he only knew in part and prophesied in part? And must it not be true of the whole Bible what the beloved apostle St. John says of his own Gospel, 'And there are many other things which Jesus did, the which if they should be written every one, I suppose that even the world itself could not contain the books that should be written?'

Bear that in mind, remembering always that the God of the Old Testament is the God of the New likewise; and whenever you read, either in the Old or New Testament, of the noble acts of the Lord, say boldly, as millions of hearts have said already, when the good news of the Bible came to them, 'This is so beautiful that it must be true. The Spirit of God in the Bible, and the judgment of the Church in all ages, bears witness with my spirit that this is true. So ought God to have done, and therefore surely so hath God done. Shall not the Judge of all the earth do RIGHT?'

DAVID:

FIVE SERMONS.

Note.—*The first four of these Sermons were preached before the University of Cambridge.*

SERMON I.

DAVID'S WEAKNESS.

He chose David his servant, and took him away from the sheep-
folds. As he was following the ewes great with young ones,
he took him; that he might feed Jacob his people, and Israel
his inheritance. So he fed them with a faithful and true heart,
and ruled them prudently with all his power.

I AM about to preach to you four sermons on
the character of David. His history, I take
for granted, you all know.

I look on David as an all but ideal king, edu-
cated for his office by an all but ideal training.
A shepherd first; a life—be it remembered—full
of danger in those times and lands; then captain
of a band of outlaws; and lastly a king, gradually
and with difficulty fighting his way to a secure
throne.

This was his course. But the most important
stage of it was probably the first. Among the

dumb animals he learnt experience which he afterwards put into practice among human beings. The shepherd of the sheep became the shepherd of men. He who had slain the lion and the bear became the champion of his native land. He who followed the ewes great with young, fed God's oppressed and weary people with a faithful and true heart, till he raised them into a great and and strong nation. So both sides of the true kingly character, the masculine and the feminine, are brought out in David. For the greedy and tyrannous, he has indignant defiance: for the weak and helpless, patient tenderness.

My motives for choosing this subject I will explain in a very few words.

We have heard much of late about 'Muscular Christianity.' A clever expression, spoken in jest by I know not whom, has been bandied about the world, and supposed by many to represent some new ideal of the Christian character.

For myself, I do not understand what it means. It may mean one of two things. If it mean the first, it is a term somewhat unnecessary, if not somewhat irreverent. If it mean the second, it means something untrue and immoral.

Its first and better meaning may be simply a

healthy and manful Christianity, one which does not exalt the feminine virtues to the exclusion of the masculine.

That certain forms of Christianity have committed this last fault cannot be doubted. The tendency of Christianity, during the patristic and the Middle Ages, was certainly in that direction. Christians were persecuted and defenceless, and they betook themselves to the only virtues which they had the opportunity of practising—gentleness, patience, resignation, self-sacrifice, and self-devotion—all that is loveliest in the ideal female character. And God forbid that that side of the Christian life should ever be undervalued. It has its own beauty, its own strength too made perfect in weakness; in prison, in torture, at the fiery stake, on the lonely sick-bed, in long years of self-devotion and resignation, and in a thousand womanly sacrifices unknown to man, but written for ever in God's book of life.

But as time went on, and the monastic life, which, whether practised by man or by woman, is essentially a feminine life, became more and more exclusively the religious ideal, grave defects began to appear in what was really too narrow a conception of the human character.

The monks of the Middle Ages, in aiming exclusively at the virtues of women, generally copied little but their vices. Their unnatural attempt to be wiser than God, and to unsex themselves, had done little but disease their mind and heart. They resorted more and more to those arts which are the weapons of crafty, ambitious, and unprincipled women. They were too apt to be cunning, false, intriguing. They were personally cowardly, as their own chronicles declare; querulous, passionate, prone to unmanly tears; prone, as their writings abundantly testify, to scold, to use the most virulent language against all who differed from them; they were, at times, fearfully cruel, as evil women will be; cruel with that worst cruelty which springs from cowardice. If I seem to have drawn a harsh picture of them, I can only answer that their own documents justify abundantly all that I have said.

Gradually, to supply their defects, another ideal arose. The warriors of the Middle Ages hoped that they might be able to serve God in the world, even in the battle-field. At least, the world and the battle-field they would not relinquish, but make the best of them. And among them arose a new and a very fair ideal of manhood: that of the "gentle, very perfect knight," loyal to his king and to his God, bound to defend the weak, succour the oppressed, and put down the wrong-doer; with his lady, or bread-giver, dealing forth bounteously the goods of this life to all who needed; occupied in the seven works of mercy, yet living in the world, and in the perfect enjoyment of wedded and family life. This was the ideal. Of course sinful human nature fell short of it, and defaced it by absurdities; but I do not hesitate to say that it was a higher ideal of Christian excellence than had appeared since the time of the Apostles, putting aside the quite exceptional ideal of the blessed martyrs.

A higher ideal, I say, was chivalry, with all its shortcomings. And for this reason: that it asserted the possibility of consecrating the whole manhood, and not merely a few faculties thereof, to God; and it thus contained the first germ of that Protestantism which conquered at the Reformation.

Then was asserted, once for all, on the grounds of nature and reason, as well as of Holy Scripture, the absolute sanctity of family and national life, and the correlative idea, namely, the consecration of the whole of human nature to the service of God, in that station to which God had called each man. Then the Old Testament, with the honour which it puts upon family and national life, became precious to man, as it had never been before; and such a history as David's became, not as it was with the mediæval monks, a mere repertory of fanciful metaphors and allegories, but the solemn example, for good and for evil, of a man of like passions and like duties with the men of the modern world.

These great truths, once asserted, could not but conquer; and they will conquer to the end. All attempts to restore the monastic and feminine ideal, like that of good Nicholas Ferrar at Little Gidding, failed. They withered like hot-house exotics in the free, keen, bracing English air; and in our civil wars, Cavalier and Puritan, in whatever they differed, never differed in their sound and healthy conviction that true religion did not crush, but strengthened and consecrated a valiant and noble manhood.

Now if all that 'Muscular Christianity' means is that, then the expression is altogether unnecessary; for we have had the thing for three centuries—and defective likewise, for it is not a merely muscular, but a human Christianity which the Bible taught our forefathers, and which our forefathers have handed down to us.

But there is another meaning sometimes attached to this flippant expression, 'Muscular Christianity,' which is utterly immoral and intolerable. There are those who say, and there have been of late those who have written books to shew, that provided a young man is sufficiently brave, frank, and gallant, he is more or less absolved from the common duties of morality and self-restraint.

That physical prowess is a substitute for virtue is certainly no new doctrine. It is the doctrine of every red man on the American prairies, of every African chief who ornaments his hut with human skulls. It was the doctrine of our heathen forefathers, when they came hither slaying, plundering, burning, tossing babes on their spear-points. But I am sorry that it should be the doctrine of any one calling himself a gentleman, much more a Christian.

It is certainly not the doctrine of the Catechism, which bids us renounce the flesh, and live by the help of God's Spirit a new life of duty to God and to our neighbour.

It is certainly not the doctrine of the New

Testament. Whatsoever St. Paul meant by bidding his disciples crucify the flesh, with its affections and lusts, he did not mean thereby that they were to deify the flesh, as the heathen round them did in their profligate mysteries and in their gladiatorial exhibitions.

Neither, though the Old Testament may seem to put more value on physical prowess than does the New Testament, is it the doctrine of the Old Testament, as I purpose to show you from the life and history of David.

Nothing, nothing, can be a substitute for purity and virtue. Man will always try to find substitutes for it. He will try to find a substitute in superstition, in forms and ceremonies, in voluntary humility and worship of angels, in using vain repetitions, and fancying that he will be heard for his much speaking; he will try to find a substitute in intellect, and the worship of intellect, and art, and poetry; or he will try to find it, as in the present case, in the worship of his own animal powers, which God meant to be his servants and not his masters. But let no man lay that flattering unction to his soul. The first and the last business of every human being, whatever his station, party, creed, capacities, tastes, duties, is morality: Virtue, Virtue, always Virtue. Nothing that man will ever invent will absolve him from the universal necessity of being good as God is good, righteous as God is righteous, and holy as God is holy.

Believe it, young men, believe it. Better would it be for any one of you to be the stupidest and the ugliest of mortals, to be the most diseased and abject of cripples, the most silly, nervous, incapable personage who ever was a laughing-stock for the boys upon the streets, if only you lived, according to your powers, the life of the Spirit of God; than to be as perfectly gifted, as exquisitely organised in body and mind as David himself, and not to live the life of the Spirit of God, the life of goodness, which is the only life fit for a human being wearing the human flesh and soul which Christ took upon him on earth, and wears for ever in heaven, a Man indeed in the midst of the throne of God.

And therefore it is, as you will yourselves have perceived already, that I have chosen to speak to you of David, his character, his history.

It is the character of a man perfectly gifted, exquisitely organised. He has personal beauty, daring, prowess, and skill in war; he has generosity, nobleness, faithfulness, chivalry as of a mediæval and Christian knight; he is a musician, poet, seemingly an architect likewise; he is, moreover, a born king; he has a marvellous and most successful power of attracting, disciplining, ruling his fellow-men. So thoroughly human a personage is he, that God speaks of him as the man after his own heart; that our blessed Lord condescends to call himself especially the Son of David.

For there is in this man (as there is said to be in all great geniuses) a feminine, as well as a masculine vein; a passionate tenderness; a keen sensibility; a vast capacity of sympathy, sadness, and suffering, which makes him truly the type of Christ, the Man of sorrows; which makes his Psalms to this day the text-book of the afflicted, of tens of thousands who have not a particle of his beauty, courage, genius; but yet can feel, in mean hovels and workhouse sick-beds, that the warrior-poet speaks to their human hearts, and for their human hearts, as none other can speak, save Christ himself, the Son of David and the Son of man.

A man, I say, of intense sensibilities; and therefore capable, as is but too notorious, of great crimes, as well as of great virtues.

And when I mention this last fact, I must ask you to pause, and consider with me very solemnly what it means.

We may pervert, or rather misstate the fact in more than one way, to our own hurt. We may say cynically, David had his good points and his bad ones, as all your great saints have. Look at them closely, and in spite of all their pretensions you will find them no better than their neighbours. And so we may comfort ourselves, in our own mediocrity and laziness, by denying the existence of all greatness and goodness.

Nathan the prophet said that David's conduct would be open to this very interpretation, and would give great occasion to the enemies of the Lord to blaspheme. But I trust that none of you wish to be numbered among the enemies of the Lord.

Again, we may say, sentimentally, that these great weaknesses are on the whole the necessary concomitants of great strength; that such highly organised and complex characters must not be judged by the rule of common respectability; and that it is a more or less fine thing to be capable at once of great virtues and great vices.

Books which hint, and more than hint this,

will suggest themselves to you at once. I only advise you not to listen to their teaching, as you will find it lead to very serious consequences, both in this life and in the life to come.

But if we do say this, or anything like this, we say it on our own responsibility. David's biographers say nothing of the kind. David himself says nothing of the kind. He never represents himself as a compound of strength and weakness. He represents himself as weakness itself—as incapacity utter and complete. To overlook that startling fact is to overlook the very element which has made David's Psalms the text-book for all human weaknesses, penitences, sorrows, struggles, aspirations, for nigh three thousand years.

But this subject is too large for me to speak of to-day; and too deep for me to attempt an explanation till I have turned your thoughts toward another object, which will explain to you David, and yourselves, and, it seems to me at times, every problem of humanity. Look not at David, but at David's greater Son; and consider Christ upon his Cross. Consider him of whom it is written, 'Thou art fairer than the children of men: full of grace are thy lips, because God hath blessed thee for ever. Gird thee with thy sword upon thy thigh, O thou most Mighty, according to thy worship and renown. Good luck have thou with thine honour; ride on, because of the word of truth, of meekness, and righteousness; and thy right hand shall teach thee terrible things. Thy arrows are very sharp, and the people shall be subdued unto thee, even in the midst among the King's enemies.' Consider him who alone fulfilled these words, who fulfils them even now eternally in heaven, King over all, God blessed for ever. And then sit down at the foot of his Cross: however young, strong, proud, gallant, gifted, ambitious you may be—sit down at the foot of Christ's Cross, and look thereon, till you see what it means, and must mean for ever. See how he nailed to that Cross, not in empty metaphor but in literal fact, in agonising soul and body, all of human nature which the world admires— youth, grace, valour, power, eloquence, intellect: not because they were evil, for he possessed them doubtless himself as did none other of the sons of men—not, I say, because they were evil, but because they were worthless and as nothing beside that divine charity which would endure and con- quer for ever, when all the noblest accidents of the body and the mind had perished, or seemed to perish. In the utmost weakness and shame of human flesh he would shew forth the strength and glory of the Divine Spirit; the strength and the glory of duty and obedience; of patience and forgiveness; of benevolence and self-sacrifice; the strength and glory of that burning love for human beings which could stoop from heaven to earth that it might seek and save that which was lost.

Yes. Look at Christ upon his Cross; the sight which melted the hearts of our fierce forefathers, and turned them from the worship of Thor and Odin to the worship of 'The white Christ;' and from the hope of a Valhalla of brute prowess, to the hope of a heaven of righteousness and love. Look at Christ upon his Cross, and see there, as they saw, the true prowess, the true valour, the true chivalry, the true glory, the true manhood, most human when most divine, which is self-sacrifice and love—as possible to the weakest, meanest, simplest, as to the strongest, most gallant, and most wise.

Look upon him, and learn from him, and take his yoke upon you, for he is meek and lowly of heart, and you shall find rest unto your souls; and in you shall be fulfilled the prophecy of Jeremiah, which he spake, saying, 'Let not the wise man glory in his wisdom, neither the mighty man glory in his might, neither let the rich man glory in his wealth: but let him that glorieth glory in this, that he understandeth and knoweth me, that I am the Lord, who exercise loving-kindness, judgment, and righteousness in the earth: for in these things I delight, saith the Lord.'

SERMON II.

DAVID'S STRENGTH.

PSALM xxvii. 1.

*The Lord is my light, and my salvation; whom then shall I fear?
The Lord is the strength of my life; of whom then shall I be
afraid?*

I SAID, last Sunday, that the key-note of David's
character was not the assertion of his own
strength, but the confession of his own weakness.
And I say it again.

But it is plain that David had strength, and
of no common order; that he was an eminently
powerful, able, and successful man. From whence
then came that strength? He says, from God.
He says, throughout his life, as emphatically as
did St. Paul after him, that God's strength was
made perfect in his weakness.

God is his deliverer, his guide, his teacher, his
inspirer. The Lord is his strength, who teaches
his hands to war, and his fingers to fight; his

hope and his fortress, his castle and deliverer, his defence, in whom he trusts; who subdueth the people that is under him.

To God he ascribes, not only his success in life, but his physical prowess. By God's help he slays the lion and the bear. By God's help he has nerve to kill the Philistine giant. By God's help he is so strong that his arms can break even a bow of steel. It is God who makes his feet like hart's feet, and enables him to leap over the walls of the mountain fortresses.

And we must pause ere we call such utterances mere Eastern metaphor. It is far more probable that they were meant as and were literal truths. David was not likely to have been a man of brute gigantic strength. So delicate a brain was probably coupled to a delicate body. Such a nature, at the same time, would be the very one most capable, under the influence—call it boldly, inspiration—of a great and patriotic cause, of great dangers and great purposes; capable, I say, at moments, of accesses of almost superhuman energy, which he ascribed, and most rightly, to the inspiration of God.

But it is not merely as his physical inspirer or protector that he has faith in God. He has a deeper, a far deeper instinct than even that; the instinct of a communion, personal, practical, living, between God, the fount of light and goodness, and his own soul, with its capacity of darkness as well as light, of evil as well as good.

In one word, David is a man of faith and a man of prayer—as God grant all you may be. It is this one fixed idea, that God could hear him, and that God would help him, which gives unity and coherence to the wonderful variety of David's Psalms. It is this faith which gives calm confidence to his views of nature and of man; and enables him to say, as he looks upon his sheep feeding round him, 'The Lord is my Shepherd, therefore I shall not want.' Faith it is which enables him to foresee that though the heathen rage, and the kings of the earth stand up, and the rulers take counsel together against the Lord and his Anointed, yet the righteous cause will surely prevail, for God is king himself. Faith it is which enables him to bear up against the general immorality, and while he cries, 'Help me, Lord, for there is not one godly man left, for the faithful fail from among the children of men'—to make answer to himself in words of noble hope and consolation, 'Now for the comfortless troubles' sake of the needy, and because of the deep sighing of the poor, I will up, saith the Lord, and will help every one from him that swelleth against him, and will set him at rest.'

Faith it is which gives a character, which no other like utterances have, to those cries of agony —cries as of a lost child—which he utters at times with such noble and truthful simplicity. They issue, almost every one of them, in a sudden counter-cry of joy as pathetic as the sorrow which has gone before. 'O Lord, rebuke me not in thine indignation: neither chasten me in thy displeasure. Have mercy upon me, O Lord, for I am weak: O Lord, heal me, for my bones are vexed. My soul also is sore troubled: but, Lord, how long wilt thou punish me? Turn thee, O Lord, and deliver my soul: O save me for thy mercy's sake. For in death no man remembereth thee: and who will give thee thanks in the pit? I am weary of my groaning; every night wash I my bed: and water my couch with my tears. My beauty is gone for very trouble: and worn away because of all mine enemies. Away from me, all ye that work vanity, for the Lord hath heard the voice of my weeping. The Lord hath heard my petition: the Lord will receive my prayer.'

Faith it is, in like wise, which gives its peculiar grandeur to that wonderful 18th Psalm, David's song of triumph; his masterpiece, and it may be the masterpiece of human poetry, inspired or un-inspired, only approached by the companion-Psalm, the 144th. From whence comes that cumulative energy, by which it rushes on, even in our translation, with a force and swiftness which are indeed divine; thought following thought, image image, verse verse, before the breath of the Spirit of God, as wave leaps after wave before the gale? What is the element in that ode, which even now makes it stir the heart like a trumpet? Surely that which it itself declares in the very first verse:

'I will love thee, O Lord, my strength; the Lord is my stony rock, and my defence: my Saviour, my God, and my might, in whom I will trust, my buckler, the horn also of my salvation, and my refuge.'

What is it which gives life and reality to the magnificent imagery of the seventh and following verses? 'The earth trembled and quaked: the very foundations also of the hills shook, and were removed, because he was wroth. There went a smoke out in his presence: and a consuming fire out of his mouth, so that coals were kindled at it. He bowed the heavens also, and came down: and it was dark under his feet. He rode upon the cherubims, and did fly: he came flying upon the wings of the wind. He made darkness his secret place: his pavilion round about him with dark water, and thick clouds to cover him. At the brightness of his presence his clouds removed: hailstones, and coals of fire. The Lord also thundered out of heaven, and the Highest gave his thunder: hailstones, and coals of fire. He sent out his arrows, and scattered them: he cast forth lightnings, and destroyed them. The springs of waters were seen, and the foundations of the round world were discovered, at thy chiding, O Lord: at the blasting of the breath of thy displeasure. He shall send down from on high to fetch me: and shall take me out of many waters.'

What protects such words from the imputation of mere Eastern exaggeration? The firm conviction that God is the deliverer, not only of David, but of all who trust in God; that the whole majesty of God, and all the powers of nature, are arrayed on the side of the good and of the oppressed. 'The Lord shall reward me after my righteous dealing: according to the cleanness of my hands shall he recompense me. Because I have kept the ways of the Lord: and have not forsaken my God, as the wicked doth. For I have an eye unto all his laws: and will not cast out his commandments from me. I was also uncorrupt before him: and eschewed mine own wickedness. Therefore shall the Lord reward me after my righteous dealing: and according unto the cleanness of my hands in his eyesight. With the holy thou shalt be holy: and with a perfect man thou shalt be perfect.'

Faith, again, it is, to turn from David's highest to his lowest phase—faith in God it is which has made that 51st Psalm the model of all true penitence for evermore. Faith in God, in the spite of his full consciousness that God is about to punish him bitterly for the rest of his life. Faith it is which gives to that Psalm its peculiarly simple, deliberate, manly tone; free from all exaggerated self-accusations, all cowardly cries of terror. He is crushed down, it is true. The tone of his words shews us that throughout. But crushed by what? By the discovery that he has offended God? Not in the least. For the sake of your own souls, as well as for that of honest critical understanding of the Scriptures, do not foist that meaning into David's words. He never says that he had offended God. Had he been a mediæval monk, had he been an average superstitious man of any creed or time, he would have said so, and cried, I have offended God; he is offended and angry with me, how shall I avert his wrath?

Not so. David has discovered not an angry, but a forgiving God; a God of love and goodness, who desires to make his creatures good. Penitential prayers in all ages have too often wanted faith in God, and therefore have been too often prayers to avert punishment. This, this—the model of all truly penitent prayers—is that of a man who is to be punished, and is content to take his punishment, knowing that he deserves it, and far more beside. And why? Because, as always, David has faith in God. God is a good and just being, and he trusts him accordingly; and that very discovery of the goodness, not the sternness of God, is the bitterest pang, the deepest shame to David's spirit. Therefore he can face without despair the discovery of a more deep, radical, inbred evil in himself than he ever expected before. 'Behold, I was shapen in wickedness: and in sin hath my mother conceived me;' because he could say also, 'Thou requirest truth in the inward parts; and shalt make me to understand wisdom secretly.' He can cry to God, out of the depths of his foulness, 'Make me a clean heart, O God: and renew a right spirit within me. Cast me not away from thy presence: and take not thy holy Spirit from me. O give me the comfort of thy help again: and stablish me with thy free Spirit. Then shall I teach thy ways unto the wicked: and sinners shall be converted unto thee.' He can cry thus, because he has discovered that the will of God is not to hate, not to torture, not to cast away from his presence, but to restore his creatures to goodness, that he may thereby restore them to usefulness. David has discovered that God demands no sacrifice, much less self-torturing penance. What he demands is the heart. The sacrifice of God is a troubled spirit. A broken and a contrite heart he will not despise.

It is such utterances as these which have given, for now many hundred years, their priceless value to the little book of Psalms ascribed to the shepherd outlaw of the Judæan hills. It is such utterances as these which have sent the sound of his name into all lands, and his words throughout all the world. Every form of human sorrow, doubt, struggle, error, sin; the nun agonising in the cloister; the settler struggling for his life in Transatlantic forests; the pauper shivering over the embers in his hovel, and waiting for kind death; the man of business striving to keep his honour pure amid the temptations of commerce; the prodigal son starving in the far country, and recollecting the words which he learnt long ago at his mother's knee; the peasant boy trudging a-field in the chill dawn, and remembering that the Lord is his shepherd, therefore he will not want—all shapes of humanity have found, and will find to the end of time, a word said to their inmost hearts, and more, a word said for those hearts to the living God of heaven, by the vast humanity of · David, the man after God's own heart; the most thoroughly human figure, as it seems to me, which had appeared upon the earth before the coming of that perfect Son of man, who is over all, God blessed for ever.   Amen.

It may be said, David's belief is no more than the common belief of fanatics. They have in all ages fancied themselves under the special protection of Deity, the object of special communications from above.

Doubtless they have; and evil conclusions have they drawn therefrom, in every age. But the existence of a counterfeit is no argument against the existence of the reality; rather it is an argument for the existence of the reality. In this case it is impossible to conceive how the idea of communion with an unseen being ever entered the human mind at all, unless it had been put there originally by fact and experience. Man would never have even dreamed of a living God, had not that living God been a reality, who did not leave the creature to find his Creator, but stooped from heaven, at the very beginning of our race, to find his creature.

And a reality you will surely find it—that living and practical communication between your souls, and that Father in heaven who created them. It will not be real, but morbid, even imaginary, just in proportion as your souls are tainted with self-conceit, ambition, self-will, malice, passion, or any wilful vice; especially with the vice of bigotry, which settles beforehand for God what he shall teach the soul, and in what manner he shall teach it, and turns a deaf ear to his plainest lessons if they cannot be made to fit into some favourite formula or theory. But it will be real, practical, healthy, soul-saving, in the very deepest sense of that word, just in proportion as your eye is single and your heart pure; just in proportion as you hunger and thirst after righteousness, and wish and try simply and humbly to do your duty in that station to which God has called you, and to learn joyfully and trustingly anything and everything which God may see fit to teach you. Then as your day your strength shall be. Then will the Lord teach you, and inform you with his eye, and guide you in the way wherein you should go. Then will you obey that appeal of the Psalmist, 'Be ye not like to horse and mule, which have no understanding, whose mouths must be held in with bit and bridle, lest they fall upon thee. Great plagues remain for the ungodly. But whoso putteth his trust in the Lord, mercy embraceth him on every side.'

For understand this well, young men, and settle it in your hearts as the first condition of human life, yea, of the life of every rational created being, that a man is justified only by faith; and not only a man, but angels, archangels, and all possible created spirits, past, present, and to come. All stand, all are in their right state, only as long as they are consciously dependent on God the Father of spirits and his Son Jesus Christ the Lord, in whom they live and move and have their being.

The moment they attempt to assert themselves, whether their own power, their own genius, their own wisdom, or even their own virtue, they *ipso facto* sin, and are justified and just no longer; because they are trying to take themselves out of their just and right state of dependence, and to put themselves into an unjust and wrong state of independence. To assert that anything is their own, to assert that their virtue is their own, just as much as to assert that their wisdom, or any other part of their being, is their own, is to deny the primary fact of their existence—that in God they live and move and have that being. And therefore Milton's Satan, though, over and above all his other grandeurs, he had been adorned with every virtue, would have been Satan still by the one sin of ingratitude, just because and just as long as he set up himself, apart from that God from whom alone comes every good and perfect gift.

Settle it in your hearts, young men, settle it in your hearts—or rather pray to God to settle it therein; and if you would love life and see good days, recollect daily and hourly that the only sane and safe human life is dependence on God himself, and that—

Unless above himself he can
Exalt himself, how poor a thing is man.

SERMON III.

DAVID'S ANGER.

Psalm cxliii. 11, 12.

Quicken me, O Lord, for thy name's sake: for thy righteousness'
sake bring my soul out of trouble. And of thy mercy cut off
mine enemies, and destroy all them that afflict my soul: for I
am thy servant.

THERE are those who would say that I dealt
unfairly last Sunday by the Psalms of David;
that in order to prove them inspired, I ignored
an element in them which is plainly uninspired,
wrong, and offensive; namely, the curses which he
invokes upon his enemies. I ignored it, they
would say, because it was fatal to my theory;
because it proved David to have the vindictive
passions of other Easterns; to be speaking, not
by the inspiration of God, but of his own private
likes and dislikes; to be at least a fanatic who
thinks that his cause must needs be God's cause,
and who invokes the lightnings of heaven on all
who dare to differ from him. Others would say

that such words were excusable in David, living under the Old Law; for it was said by them of old time, 'Thou shalt love thy neighbour and hate thine enemy:' but that our Lord has formally abrogated that permission; 'But I say unto you, Love your enemies, bless them that curse you, and do good to those who despitefully use you and persecute you.' How unnecessary, and how wrong then, they would say, it is of the Church of England to retain these cursing Psalms in her public worship, and put them into the mouths of her congregations. Either they are merely painful, as well as unnecessary to Christians; or if they mean anything, they excuse and foster the habit too common among religious controversialists of invoking the wrath of heaven on their opponents.

I argue with neither of the objectors. But the question is a curious and an important one; and I am bound, I think, to examine it in a sermon which, like the present, treats of David's chivalry.

What David meant by these curses can be best known from his own actions. What certain persons have meant by them since is patent enough from their actions. Mediæval monks considered but too often the enemies of their creed, of their ecclesiastical organisation, even of their particular monastery, to be *ipso facto* enemies of God ; and applied to them the seeming curses of David's Psalms, with fearful additions, of which David, to his honour, never dreamed. 'May they feel with Dathan and Abiram the damnation of Gehenna,'* is a fair sample of the formulæ which are found in the writings of men who, while they called themselves the servants of Jesus Christ our Lord, derived their notions of the next world principally from the sixth book of Virgil's Æneid. And what they meant by their words their acts shewed. Whenever they had the power, they were but too apt to treat their supposed enemies in this life, as they expected God to treat them in the next. The history of the Inquisition on the continent, in America, and in the Portuguese Indies—of the Marian persecutions in England— of the Piedmontese massacres in the 17th century—are facts never to be forgotten. Their horrors have been described in too authentic documents ; they remain for ever the most hideous pages in the history of sinful human nature. Do we find a hint of any similar conduct on the part

---

* From a charter quoted by Ingulf—and very probably a spurious one.

of David? If not, it is surely probable that he did not mean by his imprecations what the mediæval clergy meant.

Certainly, whatsoever likeness there may have been in language, the contrast in conduct is most striking. It is a special mark of David's character, as special as his faith in God, that he never avenges himself with his own hand. Twice he has Saul in his power : once in the cave at Engedi, once at the camp at Hachilah, and both times he refuses nobly to use his opportunity. He is his master, the Lord's Anointed ; and his person is sacred in the eyes of David his servant—his knight, as he would have been called in the Middle Age. The second time David's temptation is a terrible one. He has softened Saul's wild heart by his courtesy and pathos when he pleaded with him, after letting him escape from the cave ; and he has sworn to Saul that when he becomes king he will never cut off his children, or destroy his name out of his father's home. Yet we find Saul, immediately after, attacking him again out of mere caprice ; and once more falling into his hands. Abishai says—and who can wonder ?—'Let me smite him with the spear to the earth this once, and I will not smite a second time.' What wonder? The man is not to be trusted—truce with him is impossible; but David still keeps his chivalry, in the true meaning of that word: 'Destroy him not, for who can stretch forth his hand against the Lord's Anointed, and be guiltless? As the Lord liveth, the Lord shall smite him, or his day shall come to die; or he shall go down into battle, and perish. But the Lord forbid that I should stretch forth my hand against the Lord's Anointed.'

And if it be argued, that David regarded the person of a king as legally sacred, there is a case more clear still, in which he abjures the right of revenge upon a private person.

Nabal, in addition to his ingratitude, has insulted him with the bitterest insult which could be offered to a free man in a slave-holding country. He has hinted that David is neither more nor less than a runaway slave. And David's heart is stirred by a terrible and evil spirit. He dare not trust his men, even himself, with his black thoughts. 'Gird on your swords,' is all that he can say aloud. But he had said in his heart, 'God do so and more to the enemies of David, if I leave a man alive by the morning light of all that pertain to him.'

And yet at the first words of reason and of wisdom, urged doubtless by the eloquence of a beautiful and noble woman, but no less by the Spirit of God speaking through her, as all who call themselves gentlemen should know already, his right spirit returns to him. The chivalrous instinct of forgiveness and duty is roused once more; and he cries, 'Blessed be the Lord God of Israel, which sent thee this day to meet me; and blessed be thou, which hast kept me this day from shedding blood, and from avenging myself with mine own hand.'

It is plain then, that David's notion of his duty to his enemies was very different from that of the monks. But still they are undeniably imprecations, the imprecations of a man smarting under cruel injustice; who cannot, and in some cases must not avenge himself, and who therefore calls on the just God to avenge him. Are we therefore to say that these utterances of David are uninspired? Not in the least: we are boldly to say that they are inspired, and by the very Spirit of God, who is the Spirit of justice and of judgment.

Doubtless there were, in after ages, far higher inspirations. The Spirit of God was, and is gradually educating mankind, and individuals among mankind, like David, upward from lower truths to higher ones. That is the express assertion of our Lord and of his Apostles. But the higher and later inspiration does not make the lower and earlier false. It does not even always supersede it altogether. Each ‑is true; and, for the most part, each must remain, and be respected, that they may complement each other.

Let us look at this question rationally and reverently, free from all sentimental and immoral indulgence for sin and wrong.

The first instinct of man is the *Lex Talionis.* As you do to me—says the savage—so I have a right to do to you. If you try to kill me or mine, I have a right to kill you in return. Is this notion uninspired? I should be sorry to say so. It is surely the first form and the only possible first form of the sense of justice and retribution. As a man sows so shall he reap. If a man does wrong he deserves to be punished. No arguments will drive that great divine law out of the human mind; for God has put it there.

After that inspiration comes a higher one. The man is taught to say, I must not punish my enemy if I can avoid it. God must punish him, either by the law of the land or by his providential judgments.   To this height David rises.   In a seemingly lawless age and country, under the most extreme temptation, he learns to say, 'Blessed be God who hath kept me from avenging myself with my own hand.'

But still, it may be said, David calls down God's vengeance on his enemies.   He has not learnt to hate the sin and yet love the sinner.   Doubtless he has not: and it may have been right for his education, and for the education of the human race through him, that he did not.   It may have been a good thing for him, as a future king; it may be a good thing for many a man now, to learn the sinfulness of sin, by feeling its effects in his own person; by writhing under those miseries of body and soul, which wicked men can, and do inflict on their fellow-creatures.

There are sins which a good man will not pity, but wage internecine war against them; sins for which he is justified, if God have called him thereto, to destroy the sinner in his sins.   The traitor, the tyrant, the ravisher, the robber, the extortioner, are not objects of pity, but of punishment; and it may have been very good for David to be taught by sharp personal experience, that those who robbed the widow and put the fatherless to death, like the lawless lords of his time; those like Saul, who smote the city of the priests for having given David food—men and women, children and sucklings, oxen and asses and sheep, with the edge of the sword; those who, like the nameless traitor who so often rouses his indignation—his own familiar friend who lifted up his heel against him—sought men's lives under the guise of friendship: that such, I say, were persons not to be tolerated upon the face of God's earth. We do not tolerate them now. We punish them by law. We even destroy them wholesale in war, without inquiring into their individual guilt or innocence. David was taught, not by abstract meditation in his study, but by bitter need and agony, not to tolerate them then. If he could have destroyed them as we do now, it is not for us to say that he would have been wrong. And what if he were indignant, and what if he expressed that indignation? I have yet to discover that indignation against wrong is aught but righteous, noble, and divine. The flush of rage and scorn which rises, and ought to rise in every honest heart, when we see a woman or a child ill-used, a poor man wronged or crushed— What is that, but the inspiration of Almighty

God? What is that but the likeness of Christ?
Woe to the man who has lost that feeling! Woe
to the man who can stand coolly by, and see
wrong done without a shock or a murmur, or even
more, to the very limits of the just laws of this
land. He may think it a fine thing so to do; a
proof that he is an· easy, prudent man of the
world, and not a meddlesome enthusiast. But
all that it does prove is: That the Spirit of God,
who is the Spirit of justice and judgment, has
departed from him.

I say the Spirit of God and the likeness of
Christ. Instead of believing David's own statement of the wrong doings of these men about
him, we may say cynically, and as it seems to
me most unfairly, 'Of course there were two
sides to David's quarrels, as there are to all such;
and of course he took his own side; and considered himself always in the right, and every
one who differed from him in the wrong;' and
such a speech will sound sufficiently worldly-wise
to pass for philosophy with some critics; but,
unfortunately, he who says that of David, will
be bound in all fairness to say it of our Lord
Jesus Christ.

For you must remember that there was a class

of sinners in Judæa, to whom our Lord speaks no word of pity or forgiveness: namely, the very men who were his own personal enemies, who were persecuting him, and going about to kill him; and that therefore, by any hard words toward them, he must have laid himself open, just as much as David laid himself open, to the imputation of personal spite. And yet, what did he say to the scribes and Pharisees: 'Ye go about to kill me, and therefore I am bound to say nothing harsh concerning you'? What he did say was this: 'Ye serpents, ye generation of vipers, how can ye escape the damnation of hell?' .

Yes; in the Son of David, as in David's self, there was, and is, and will be for ever and ever, no weak, and really cruel indulgence; but a burning fire of indignation against all hypocrisy, tyranny, lust, cruelty, and every other sin by which men oppress, torment, deceive, degrade their fellow-men; and still more, still more, remember that, all young men, their fellow-women. That fire burns for ever—the Divine fire of God; the fire not of hatred, but of love to mankind, which will therefore punish, and if need be, exterminate all who shall dare to make mankind the worse, whether in body or soul or mind.

But David prays God to kill his enemies. No doubt he does. Probably they deserved to be killed. He does not ask, you will always remember, if you be worthy of the name of critical students of the Bible—he does not ask, as did the mediæval monks, that his enemies should go to endless torments after they died. True or false, that is a more modern notion—and if it be applied to the Psalms, an interpolation—of which David knew nothing. He asks simply that the men may die. Probably he knew his own business best, and the men deserved to die ; to be killed either by God .or by man, as do too many in all ages.

If we take the Bible as it stands (and we have no right to do otherwise), these men were trying to kill David. He could not, and upon a point of honour, would not kill them himself. But he believed, and rightly, that God can punish the offender whom man cannot touch, and that He will, and does punish them. And if he calls on God to execute justice and judgment upon these men, he only calls on God to do what God is doing continually on the face of the whole earth. In fact, God does punish here, in this life. He does not, as false preachers say, give over this life to impunity, and this world to the devil, and only resume the reins of moral government and the right of retribution when men die and go into the next world. Here, in this life, he punishes sin; slowly, but surely, God punishes. And if any of you doubt my words, you have only to commit sin, and then see whether your sin will find you out.

The whole question turns on this, Are we to believe in a living God, or are we not? If we are not, then David's words are of course worse than nothing. If we are, I do not see why David was wrong in calling on God to exercise that moral and providential government of the world, which is the very note and definition of a living God.

But what right have we to use these words? My friends, if the Church bids us use these words, she certainly does not bid us act upon them. She keeps them, I believe most rightly, as a record of a human experience, which happily seems to us special and extreme, of which we, in a well-governed Christian land, know nothing, and shall never know.

Special and extreme? Alas, alas! In too many countries, in too many ages, it has been the common, the almost universal experience of the many weak, enslaved, tortured, butchered at the wicked will of the few strong.

There have been those in tens of thousands, there may be those again who will have a right to cry to God, 'Of thy goodness slay mine enemies, lest they slay, or worse than slay, both me and mine.' There were thousands of English after the Norman Conquest; there were thousands of Hindoos in Oude before its annexation; there are thousands of negroes at this moment in their native land of Africa, crushed and outraged by hereditary tyrants, who had and have a right to appeal to God, as David appealed to him against the robber lords of Palestine; a right to cry, 'Rid us, O God; if thou be a living God, a God of justice and mercy, rid us not only of these men, but of their children after them. This tyrant, stained with lust and wine and blood; this robber chieftain who privily in his lurking dens murders the innocent, and ravishes the poor when he getteth him into his net; this slave-hunting king who kills the captives whom he cannot sell; and whose children after him will inevitably imitate his cruelties and his rapine and treacheries— deal with him and his as they deserve. Set an ungodly man to be ruler over him; that he may find out what we have been enduring from his ungodly rule. Let his days be few, and another take his office. Let his children be fatherless, and his wife a widow. Let his children beg their bread out of desolate places. Let there be no man to pity him or take compassion on his fatherless children—to take his part, and breed up a fresh race of tyrants to our misery. Let the extortioner consume all he hath, and the stranger spoil his labour—for what he has is itself taken by extortion, and he has spoiled the labour of thousands. Let his posterity be destroyed, and in the next generation his name be clean put out. Let the wickedness of his father and the sin of his mother be had in remembrance in the sight of the Lord; that he may root out the memorial of them from the earth, and enable law and justice, peace and freedom to take the place of anarchy and tyranny and blood.'

That prayer was answered—if we are to believe the records of Norman, not English, monks in England after the Conquest, by the speedy extinction of the most guilty families among the Norman conquerors. It is being answered, thank God, in Hindostan at this moment. It will surely

be answered in Africa in God's good time ; for the
Lord reigneth, be the nations never so unquiet.
And we, if we will read such words rationally
and humanly, remembering the state of society
in which they were written—a state of society,
alas ! which has endured, and still endures over
a vast portion of the habitable globe ; where might
is right, and there is little or no principle, save
those of lust and greed and revenge—then instead
of wishing such words out of the Bible, we shall
be glad to keep them there, as testimonies to the
moral government of the world by a God and a
Christ who will surely avenge the innocent blood ;
and as a Gospel of comfort to suffering millions,
when the news reaches them at last, that they
may call on God to deliver them from their tor-
mentors, and that he will hear their cry, and will
help them.

SERMON IV.

DAVID'S DESERTS.

2 SAMUEL i. 26.

I am distressed for thee, my brother Jonathan: very pleasant
hast thou been unto me: thy love to me was wonderful, passing
the love of women.

PASSING the love of woman? How can that
be, we of these days shall say. What love
can pass that, saving the boundless love of him
who stooped from heaven to earth, that he might
die on the Cross for us? No. David, when he
sang those words, knew not the depth of woman's
love. And we shall have a right so to speak. The
indefeasible and Divine right which is bestowed
by fact.

As a fact, we do not find among the ancient
Jews that exalting and purifying ideal of the
relations between man and woman, which is to
be found, thank God, in these days, in almost
every British work of fiction or fancy.

It is enunciated, remember always, in the oldest

Hebrew document. On the very threshold of the Bible, in the very first chapters of Genesis, it is enunciated in its most ideal purity and perfection. But in practice it was never fulfilled. No man seems to have attempted to fulfil it. Man becomes a polygamist, lower than the very birds of the air. Abraham, the father of the faithful, has his Sarah, his princess-wife: but he has others beside, as many as he will. And so has David in like wise, to the grief and harm of both him and Abraham.

So, it would seem, had the majority of the Jews till after the Captivity; and even then the law of divorce seems to have been as indulgent toward the man as it was unjust and cruel toward the woman. Then our blessed Lord reasserted the ideal and primæval law. He testified in behalf of woman, the puppet of a tyrant who repudiated her upon the most frivolous pretext, and declared that in the beginning God made them male and female; the one husband for the one wife. But his words fell on unwilling ears. His disciples answered, that if the case of a man with his wife be such, it is not good for a man to marry. And such, as a fact, was the general opinion of Christendom for many centuries.

But of that, as of other sayings of our Lord's, were his own words fulfilled, that the kingdom of God is as if a man should put seed into the ground, and sleep and wake, and the seed should spring up, and bear fruit, he knew not how.

In due course of time, when the Teutonic nations were Christianised, there sprang up among them an idea of married love, which showed that our Lord's words had at last fallen on good ground, and were destined to bear fruit an hundredfold.

Gradually, with many confusions, and sometimes sinful mistakes, there arose, not in the cloister, not in the study—not even, alas! in the churches of God, as they were then; but in the flowery meads of May; under the forest boughs, where birds sang to their mates; by the side of the winter hearth; from the lips of wandering minstrels; in the hearts of young creatures, whom neither the profligacy of worldlings, nor the prudery of monks, had yet defiled: from them arose a voice, most human and yet most divine, reasserting once more the lost law of Eden, and finding in its fulfilment, strength and purity, self-sacrifice and self-restraint.

That voice grew clearer and more strong as time went on. It was purged from youthful mistakes and youthful grossnesses; till, at the Reformation, it could speak clearly, fully, once and for all—no longer on the ground of mere nature and private fancy, but on the ground of Scripture, and reason, and the eternal laws of God; and the highest ideal of family life became possible to the family and to the nation, in proportion as they accepted the teaching of the Reformation: and impossible, alas! in proportion as they still allowed themselves to be ruled by a priesthood who asserted the truly monstrous dogma, that the sexes reach each their highest excellence only when parted from each other.

But these things were hidden from David. One can well conceive that he, so gifted outwardly and inwardly, must have experienced all that was then possible of woman's love. In one case, indeed, he was notably brought under that moral influence of woman, which we now regard and rightly, as one of the holiest influences of this life. The scene is unique in Scripture. It reads like a scene out of the Middle Age.

Abigail's meeting with David under the covert of the hill; her turning him from his purpose of wild revenge by graceful compliments, by the frank, and yet most modest expression of her sympathy and admiration ; and David's chivalrous answer to her chivalrous appeal—all that scene, which painters have so often delighted to draw, is a fore-feeling, a prophecy, as it were, of the Christian chivalry of after ages. The scene is most human and most divine: and we are not shocked to hear that after Nabal's death the fair and rich lady joins her fortune to that of the wild outlaw, and becomes his wife to wander by wood and wold.

But amid all the simple and sacred beauty of that scene, we cannot forget, we must not forget that Abigail is but one wife of many ; that there is an element of pure, single, all-absorbing love absent at least in David's heart, which was present in the hearts of our forefathers in many a like case, and which they have handed down to us as an heirloom, as precious as that of our laws and liberties.

And all this was sin unto David ; and like all sin, brought with it its own punishment. I do not mean to judge him : to assign his exact amount of moral responsibility. Our Lord forbids us positively to do that to any man ; and least of all, to a man who only acted according to his right, and the fashion of his race and his age.

But we must fix it very clearly in our minds, that sins may be punished in this life, even though he who commits them is not aware that they are sins. If you are ignorant that fire burns, your ignorance will not prevent your hand from suffering if you put it into the fire. If you are of opinion that two and two make five, and therefore spend five pounds while you only possess four, your mistake will not prevent your being in debt. And so with all mortal affairs.

Sin, ἁμάρτια, means first, it seems to me, a missing the mark, end, or aim of our existence; a falling short of the law, the ideal, the good works which God has prepared beforehand for us to walk in; and every such sin, conscious or unconscious, must avenge itself by the Divine laws of the universe, whether physical or spiritual. No miracle is needed; no intervention of God with his own laws. His laws are far too well made for him to need to break them a second time, because a sinner has broken them already. They avenge themselves. And so does polygamy. So it did in the case of David. It is a breach of the ideal law of human nature; and he who breaks that law must suffer, as David suffered.

Look at the latter history of David, and at

what it might have been. One can conceive so noble a personage under such woman's influence as, thank God, is common now, going down into an honoured old age, and living together with a helpmate worthy of him in godly love and honesty to his life's end; seeing his children Christianly and virtuously brought up, to the praise and honour of God.

And what was the fact?

The indulgence of his passions — seemingly harmless to him at first—becomes most harmful ere he dies. He commits a crime, or rather a complication of crimes, which stains his name for ever among men.

I do not think that we shall understand that great crime of David's, if we suppose it, with some theologians, to have been merely a sudden and solitary fall, from which he recovered by repentance, and became for the time to come as good a man as he had ever been. Such a theory, however well it may fit certain theological systems, does not fit the facts of human life, or, as I hold, the teaching of Scripture.

Such terrible crimes are not committed by men in a right state of mind. *Nemo repente fuit turpissimus.* He who commits adultery, treachery, and murder, must have been long tampering, at least in heart, with all these. Had not David been playing upon the edge of sin, into sin he would not have fallen.

He may have been quite unconscious of bad habits of mind; but they must have been there, growing in secret. The tyrannous self-will, which is too often developed by long success and command: the unscrupulous craft, which is too often developed by long adversity, and the necessity of sustaining oneself in a difficult position—these must have been there. But even they would not have led David to do the deed which he did, had there not been in him likewise that fearful moral weakness which comes from long indulgence of the passions—a weakness which is reckless alike of conscience, of public opinion, and of danger either to earthly welfare or everlasting salvation.

It has been said, 'But such a sin is so unlike David's character.' Doubtless it was, on the theory that David was a character mingled of good and evil. But on David's own theory, that he was an utterly weak person without the help of God, the act is perfectly like David. It is David's self. It is what David would naturally do when he had left hold of God. Had he left hold of God in the wilderness he would have become a mere robber-chieftain. He does leave hold of God in his palace on Zion, and he becomes a mere Eastern despot.

And what of his sons?

The fearful curse of Nathan, that the sword shall never depart from his house, needs, as usual, no miracle to fulfil it. It fulfils itself. The tragedies of his sons, of Amnon, of Absalom, are altogether natural—to have been foreseen, but not to have been avoided.

The young men have seen their father put no restraint upon his passions. Why should they put restraint on theirs? How can he command them when he has not commanded himself? And yet self-restraint is what they, above all men, need. Upstart princes—the sons of a shepherd boy—intoxicated with honours to which they were not born; they need the severest discipline; they break out into the most frantic licence. What is there that they may not do, and dare not do? Nothing is sacred in their eyes. Luxury, ambition, revenge, vanity, recklessness of decency, open rebellion, disgrace them in the sight of all men. And all these vices, remember, are heightened by the fact that they are not brothers, but rivals; sons of different mothers, hating each other, plotting against each other; each, probably, urged on by his own mother, who wishes, poor fool, to set up her son as a competitor for the throne against all the rest. And so are enacted in David's house those tragedies which have disgraced, in every age, the harems of Eastern despots.

But most significant is the fact, that those tragedies complete themselves by the sin and shame of David's one virtuous and famous son. Significant truly, that in his old age Solomon the wise should love strange women, and deserting for their sakes the God of his fathers, end as an idolater and a dotard, worshipping the abominations of the heathen, his once world-famous wisdom sunk into utter folly.

But, it may be said, the punishment of David's sin fell on his sons, and not upon himself.

How so? Can there be a more heavy punishment, a more bitter pain, than to be punished in and by his children; to see his own evil example working out their shame and ruin? But do not fancy that David's own character did not suffer for his sin. The theory that he became, instantly on his repentance, as good and great a man as he was before his fall, was convenient enough to certain theologians of past days; but it is neither warranted by the facts of Scripture, nor by the noble agonies, however noble, of the 51st Psalm.

It is a prayer for restoration, and that of the only right and true kind: 'Take not thy Holy Spirit from me;' and, as such, it was doubtless heard: but it need not have been fulfilled instantly and at once. It need not have been fulfilled, it may be, till that life to come, of which David knew so little. It is a fact, it was not fulfilled in this life. We read henceforth of no noble and heroical acts of David. From that time forth—I speak with all diffidence, and merely as it seems to me—he is a broken man. His attitude in Absalom's rebellion is all but imbecile. No act is recorded of him to the day of his death but what is questionable, if not mean and crafty. The one sudden flash of the old nobleness which he has shewn in pardoning Shimei, he himself stultifies with his dying lips by a mean command to Solomon to entrap and slay the man whom he has too rashly forgiven. The whole matter of the sacrifice of Saul's sons is so very strange, so puzzling, even shocking to our ideas of right and wrong, 'that I cannot wonder at, though I dare not endorse, Coleridge's bold assertion, that they were sacrificed to a plot of State policy, and the suspicion of some critics, that the whole scene was arranged between David and a too complaisant priesthood, and God's name blasphemously taken in vain to find a pretext for a political murder. And so David shivers pitiably to his grave, after a fashion which has furnished a jest for cynics and infidels, but which contains, to the eyes of a wise man, the elements of the deepest tragedy; one more awful lesson that human. beauty, valour, wit, genius, success, glory, are vanity of vanities : that man is nothing, and God is all in all.

But some may ask, What has all this to do with us? To do with us? Do you think that the Scripture says in vain, 'All these things are written for our example'? As long as human nature is what it is now, and was three thousand years ago, so long shall we be tempted to commit the same sins as David : different in outward form, according to the conditions of society; but the same in spirit, the same in sinfulness, and the same in the sure punishment which they bring. And above all, will men to the end be tempted to the sin of self-indulgence, want of self-control. In many ways, but surely in some way or other, will every man's temptation be, to lose self-control.

Therefore settle it in your minds, young men, that the first and the last of all virtues and graces of which God can give is self-control; as necessary for the saint and the sage, lest they become fanatics or pedants, as for the young man in the hey-day of youth and health; but as necessary for the young man as for the saint and the sage, lest, while they become only fanatics and pedants, he become a profligate, and a cumberer of the ground.

Remember this — remember it now in the glorious days of youth which never will return, but in which you are sowing seed of which you will reap the fruit until your dying day. Know that as you sow, so will you reap. If you sow to the flesh, you will of the flesh reap corruption; corruption—deterioration, whether of health, of intellect, of character in some shape or other. You know not, and no man knows, what the curse will be like; but the curse will surely come. The thing which is done cannot be undone; and you will find that out before, and not merely after your dying day. Therefore rejoice in your youth, for God has given it to you; but remember, that for it, as for each and all of his gifts, God will bring you into judgment. And when the hour of temptation comes, go back—go back, if you would escape—to what you all were taught at your mother's knee concerning the grace of God; for that alone will keep you safe, or angel, or archangel, or any created being safe, in this life and in all lives to come.

SERMON V.

FRIENDSHIP; OR, DAVID AND JONATHAN.

2 SAMUEL I. 26.

I am distressed for thee, my brother Jonathan : very pleasant hast
thou been unto me : thy love to me was wonderful, passing the
love of women.

PASSING the love of woman! That is a
hard saying. What love can pass that? Yet
David doubtless spoke truth. He was a man
who must have had reason enough to know what
woman's love was like; and when he said that
the love of Jonathan for him passed even that, he
bestowed on his friend praise which will be immortal.

The name of Jonathan will remain for ever as
the perfect pattern of friendship.

Let us think a little to-day over his noble
character and his tragical history. It will surely
do us good. If it does nothing but make us
somewhat ashamed of ourselves, that is almost the
best thing which can happen to us or to any man.

We first hear of Jonathan as doing a very gallant deed. We might expect as much. It is only great-hearted men who can be true friends; mean and cowardly men can never know what friendship means.

The Israelites were hidden in thickets, and caves, and pits, for fear of the Philistines, when Jonathan was suddenly inspired to attack a Philistine garrison, under circumstances seemingly desperate. 'And that first slaughter, which Jonathan and his armour-bearer made, was about twenty men, within, as it were, an half-acre of land, which a yoke of oxen might plough.'

That is one of those little hints which shews that the story is true, written by a man who knew the place—who had probably been in the great battle of Beth-aven, which followed, and had perhaps ascended the rock where Jonathan had done his valiant deed, and had seen the dead bodies lying as they had fallen before him and his armour-bearer.

Then follows the story of David's killing Goliath, and coming back to Saul with the giant's head in his hand, and answering modestly to him, 'I am the son of thy servant Jesse the Bethlehemite.'

'And it came to pass, when he had made an end of speaking unto Saul, that the soul of Jonathan was knit with the soul of David, and Jonathan loved him as his own soul.

'Then Jonathan and David made a covenant, because he loved him as his own soul.

'And Jonathan stripped himself of the robe that was upon him, and gave it to David, and his garments, even to his sword, and to his bow, and to his girdle.'

He loved him as his own soul. And why? Because his soul was like the soul of David; because he was modest, he loved David's modesty; because he was brave, he loved David's courage; because he was virtuous, he loved David's virtue. He saw that David was all that he was himself, and more; and therefore he loved him as his own soul. And therefore I said, that it is only noble and great hearts who can have great friendships; who admire and delight in other men's goodness; who, when they see a great and godlike man, conceive, like Jonathan, such an affection for him that they forget themselves, and think only of him, till they will do anything for him, sacrifice anything for him, as Jonathan did for David.

For remember, that Jonathan had cause to hate

and envy David rather than love him; and that he would have hated him if there had been any touch of meanness or selfishness in his heart. Gradually he learnt, as all Israel learnt, that Samuel had anointed David to be king, and that he, Jonathan, was in danger of not succeeding after Saul's death. David stood between him and the kingdom. And yet he did not envy David— did not join his father for a moment in plotting his ruin. He would oppose his father, secretly indeed, and respectfully; but still, he would be true to David, though he had to bear insults and threats of death.

And mark here one element in Jonathan's great friendship. Jonathan is a pious man, as well as a righteous one. He believes the Lord's messages that he has chosen David to be king, and he submits; seeing that it is just and right, and that David is worthy of the honour, though it be to the hurt of himself and of his children after him. It is the Lord's will; and he, instead of repining against it, must carry it out as far as he is concerned. Yes; those who are most true to their fellow-men are always those who are true to God; for the same spirit of God which makes them fear God makes them also love their neighbour.

When David escapes from Saul to Samuel, it is Jonathan who does all he can to save him. The two friends meet secretly in the field.

'And Jonathan said unto David, O Lord God of Israel, when I have sounded my father about to-morrow any time, or the third day, and, behold, if there be good toward David, and I then send not unto thee, and shew it thee; the Lord do so and much more to Jonathan.'

Then David and Jonathan agree upon a sign between them, by which David may know Saul's humour without his bow-bearer finding out David. He will shoot three arrows toward the place where David is in hiding; and if he says to his bow-bearer, The arrows are on this side of thee, David is to come; for he is safe. But if he says, The arrows are beyond thee, David must flee for his life, for the Lord has sent him away.

Then Jonathan goes in to meat with his father Saul, and excuses David for being absent.

'Then Saul's anger was kindled against Jonathan, and he said unto him, Thou son of the perverse, rebellious woman, do not I know that thou hast chosen the son of Jesse to thine own confusion, and unto the confusion of thy mother? For as long as the son of Jesse liveth upon the ground, thou shalt not be established, nor thy kingdom. Wherefore now send and fetch him unto me, for he shall surely die. And Jonathan answered Saul his father, and said unto him, Wherefore shall he be slain? what hath he done? And Saul cast a javelin at him to smite him; whereby Jonathan knew that it was determined of his father to slay David.'

He goes to the field and shoots the arrows, and gives the sign agreed on. He sends his bow-bearer back to the city, and David comes out of his hiding-place in the rock Ezel.

'And as soon as the lad was gone, David arose out of a place toward the south, and fell on his face to the ground, and bowed himself three times; and they kissed one another, and wept one with another, until David exceeded. And Jonathan said to David, Go in peace, forasmuch as we have sworn both of us in the name of the Lord, saying, The Lord be between me and thee, and between my seed and thy seed for ever. And he arose and departed: and Jonathan went into the city.'

And so the two friends parted, and saw one another, it seems, but once again, when Jonathan went to David in the forest of Ziph, and 'strength-ened his hand in God,' with noble words.

After that, Jonathan vanishes from the story of David. We hear only of him that he died fighting by his father's side, upon the downs of Gilboa. The green plot at their top, where the Israelites' last struggle was probably made, can be seen to this day; and there most likely Jonathan fell, and over him David raised his famous lamentation:

'O Jonathan, thou wast slain in thine high places. I am distressed for thee, my brother Jonathan: very pleasant hast thou been unto me: thy love to me was wonderful, passing the love of women. How are the mighty fallen, and the weapons of war perished!'

So ends the beautiful and tragical story of a truly gallant man. Seldom, indeed, will there be seen in the world such perfect friendship between man and man, as that between Jonathan and David. Seldom, indeed, shall we see anyone loving and adoring the very man whom his selfish interest would teach him to hate and to supplant. But still every man may have, and ought to have a friend. Wretched indeed, and probably deservedly wretched, is the man who has none. And every man may learn from this story of Jonathan how to choose his friends.

I say, to choose. No one is bound to be at the mercy of anybody and everybody with whom he may come in contact. No one is bound to say, That man lives next door to me, therefore he must be my friend. We are bound not to avoid our neighbours. They are put near us by God in his providence. God intends every one of them, good or bad, to help in educating us, in giving us experience of life and manners. We are to learn from them, live with them in peace and charity, and only avoid them when we find that their company is really doing us harm, and leading us into sin and folly. But a friend—which is a much deeper and more sacred word than neighbour—a friend we have the right and the power to choose; and our wisest plan will be to copy Jonathan, and choose our friends, not for their usefulness, but for their goodness; not for their worth to us, but for their worth in themselves; and to choose, if possible, people superior to ourselves. If we meet a man better than ourselves, more wise than ourselves, more learned, more experienced, more delicate-minded, more high-minded, let us take pains to win his esteem, to gain his confidence, and to win him as a friend, for the sake of his worth.

Then in our friendship, as in everything else in the world, we shall find the great law come true, that he that loseth his life shall save it. He who does not think of himself and his own interest will be the very man who will really help himself, and further his own interest the most.

For the friend whom we have chosen for his own worth, will be the one who will be worth most to us. The friend whom we have loved and admired for his own sake, will be the one who will do most to raise our character, to teach us, to refine us, to help us in time of doubt and trouble. The higher-minded man our friend is, the higher-minded will he make us. For it is written, 'As iron sharpeneth iron, so a man sharpeneth the face of his friend.'

Nothing can be more foolish, or more lowering to our own character, than to choose our friends among those who can only flatter us, and run after us, who look up to us as oracles, and fetch and carry at our bidding, while they do our souls and characters no good, but merely feed our self-conceit, and lower us down to their own level. But it is wise, and ennobling to our own character, to choose our friends among those who are nearer to God than we are, more experienced in life, and

more strong and settled in character. Wise it is
to have a friend of whom we are at first somewhat afraid; before whom we dare not say or do
a foolish thing, whose just anger or contempt
would be to us a thing terrible. Better it is that
friendship should begin with a little wholesome
fear, till time and mutual experience of each
other's characters shall have brought about the
perfect love which casts out fear. Better to say
with David, ' He that telleth lies shall not stay in
my sight; I will not know a wicked person. Yea,
let the righteous rather smite me friendly and
reprove me. All my delight is in the saints that
are in the earth, and in such as excel in virtue.'

And let no man fancy that by so doing he lowers
himself, and puts himself in a mean place. There
is no man so strong-minded but what he may
find a stronger-minded man than himself to give
him counsel; no man is so noble-hearted but what
he may find a nobler-hearted man than himself to
keep him up to what is true and just and honourable, when he is tempted to play the coward, and
be false to God's Spirit within him. No man is
so pure-minded but what he may find a purer-
minded person than himself to help him in the
battle against the world, the flesh, and the devil.

My friends, do not think it a mean thing to look up to those who are superior to yourselves. On the contrary, you will find in practice that it is only the meanest hearts, the shallowest and the basest, who feel no admiration, but only envy for those who are better than themselves; who delight in finding fault with them, and blackening their character, and showing that they are not, after all, so much superior to other people; while it is the noblest-hearted, the very men who are most worthy to be admired themselves, who, like Jonathan, feel most the pleasure, the joy, and the strength of reverence; of having some one whom they can look up to and admire; some one in whose company they can forget themselves, their own interest, their own pleasure, their own honour and glory, and cry, Him I must hear; him I must follow; to him I must cling, whatever may betide.

Blessed and ennobling is the feeling which gathers round a wise teacher or a great statesman all the most earnest, high-minded, and pious youths of his generation; the feeling which makes soldiers follow the general whom they trust, they know not why or whither, through danger, and hunger, and fatigue, and death itself; the feeling which, in its highest perfection, made the Apostles forsake all and follow Christ, saying, 'Lord, to whom shall we go? Thou hast the words of eternal life'—which made them ready to work and to die for him whom the world called the son of the carpenter, but whom they, through the Spirit of God bearing witness with their own pure and noble spirits, knew to be the Son of the Living God.

Ay, a blessed thing it is for any man or woman to have a friend; one human soul whom we can trust utterly; who knows the best and the worst of us, and who loves us, in spite of all our faults; who will speak the honest truth to us, while the world flatters us to our face, and laughs at us behind our back; who will give us counsel and reproof in the day of prosperity and self-conceit; but who, again, will comfort and encourage us in the day of difficulty and sorrow, when the world leaves us alone to fight our own battle as we can.

If we have had the good fortune to win such a friend, let us do anything rather than lose him. We must give and forgive; live and let live. If our friend have faults, we must bear with them. We must hope all things, believe all things, endure all things, rather than lose that most precious of all earthly possessions—a trusty friend.

And a friend, once won, need never be lost, if we will only be trusty and true ourselves. Friends may part—not merely in body, but in spirit, for a while. In the bustle of business and the accidents of life they may lose sight of each other for years; and more—they may begin to differ in their success in life, in their opinions, in their habits, and there may be, for a time, coldness and estrangement between them; but not for ever, if each will be but trusty and true.

For then, according to the beautiful figure of the poet, they will be like two ships who set sail at morning from the same port, and ere nightfall lose sight of each other, and go each on its own course, and at its own pace, for many days, through many storms and seas; and yet meet again, and find themselves lying side by side in the same haven, when their long voyage is past.

And if not, my friends; if they never meet; if one shall founder and sink upon the seas, or even change his course, and fly shamefully home again: still, is there not a Friend of friends who cannot change, but is the same yesterday, to-day, and for ever?

What says the noble hymn:—

> ' When gathering clouds around I view,
> And days are dark and friends are few,
> On him I lean, who, not in vain,
> Experienced every human pain :
> He sees my griefs, allays my fears,
> And counts and treasures up my tears.'

Passing the love of woman was his love, indeed; and of him Jonathan was but such a type, as the light in the dewdrop is the type of the sun in heaven.

He himself said—and what he said, that he fulfilled—'Greater love hath no man than this—that a man lay down his life for his friends.'

In treachery and desertion; in widowhood and childlessness; in the hour of death, and in the day of judgment, when each soul must stand alone before its God, one Friend remains, and that the best of all.

J. PALMER, PRINTER, 23, JESUS LANE, CAMBRIDGE.